c. jeff woods

congregational
MEGATRENDS

LINCOLN CHRISTIAN COLLEGE AND SEMINARY

an alban institute publication

The Publication Program of The Alban Institute is assisted by a grant from
Trinity Church, New York City.

Library of Congress Catalog Card Number 95-83891
ISBN #1-56699-165-X

TABLE OF CONTENTS

Gratis

90709

ACKNOWLEDGMENTS

I appreciate the wonderful support and encouragement of my family, Kandy, Brandon, and Kelsey. My gratitude goes once again to Celia Hahn and Evelyn Bence for their editing expertise and assistance.

INTRODUCTION

Someday you will have the opportunity to look back and say that you lived during a time when the church entered a new era. The church is changing shape. The church is transforming. It is changing the way it worships, grows, ministers, and educates. Like it or not, you are a part of that change.

Chances are, you have heard others mention the fact that the church is changing. Maybe your pastor has alluded to some changes. Possibly you have attended a conference that opened the door to changes. Maybe you have experienced changes in your congregation.

Wouldn't you like an opportunity to talk about the changes taking place in your congregation? Wouldn't you like an opportunity to mold some of the changes for your particular congregation?

This book is written as a resource to help pastors and laity (1) talk about the changes transpiring in congregations and (2) shape a new congregation for the future. I have detailed seven aspects of congregations and tried to show how each aspect is changing. Each chapter contains a "Where We Begin" section detailing both questions for discussion and ideas for implementation.

Megatrends in our congregations are redefining the way we do evangelism, discipleship, and ministry. Megatrends are redefining the way we view spirituality, leadership, programming, and planning. The seven megatrends that I see arising in our congregations are:

- a shift from mass evangelism to relational evangelism
- a shift from tribal education to immigrant education
- a shift from surrogate missions to hands-on missions
- a shift from reasonable spirituality to mysterious spirituality

- a shift from official leadership to gifted leadership
- a shift from segmented programming to holographic programming
- a shift from secondary planning to primary planning

Churches in America are in the midst of a major transition. The changes taking place in our churches are more significant than merely individual trends. Collectively, the trends serve to shape a whole new way of being church in America.

I have taken a snapshot of the changes I see taking place in American congregations. Prior to presenting a chapter on each of the seven megatrends, I will provide some background information revealing how our congregations entered into a period of transition in the first place. I do not claim to have all the answers. Each chapter details the background of each trend, providing evidence from statistics, theories, practitioners, and scripture. Your church will not have experienced all of these megatrends to the same degree. Some you may have not experienced at all. Others you may wish to relabel or redefine.

The goal of this book is not to say, "This is absolutely the way things are," or, "This is precisely the church of the future." Rather, the goal is to provide some material for discussion among pastors and laity about changes in our congregations. As discussions occur, I hope congregations will become more proactive than reactive regarding the future shape of American congregations. I believe that each change has a potential positive effect, but only if we stress the benefits rather than the shortcomings of each change. To do this, we must have knowledge.

I invite you to read about the changes in our congregations. Read, reflect, write in the margins, answer the discussion questions, jot down other questions, and have fun planning what your congregation will look like in the next century.

PART 1

Forming the Basis for the Megatrends

All our dreams can come true—
if we have the courage to pursue them.

Walt Disney

CHAPTER ONE

The Church Is Changing

Futurists have predicted it. Philosophers have pondered it. Pastors have reacted to it. Church members have experienced it. I'm talking about the SHIFT. The CHANGE. The dramatic movements that are taking place in our churches.

Things don't work like they used to. The church is changing. Evangelism is different. Discipleship is different. Ministry is different. People don't come to church for the same reasons they once did. People don't worship like they used to. People don't have the same loyalties, the same devotion, or the same sense of spirituality. At times, everything in the church appears to be different.

Predicting the Future

Imagine being alive a hundred years ago and trying to predict what society would be like today. A man named John Elfreth Watkins sat down at his desk and did just that. In 1900 he hypothesized about our times—what life would be like in the year 2001.[1] Even though Watkins was wise enough to predict beyond the span of his lifetime, so he would be long gone before others could judge his predictions, he did quite well with his venturesome spirit. Now that the year 2001 is much closer to us than the year 1900, it is fascinating to see just how accurate many of Watkins's predictions were.

Watkins predicted that people would be one to two inches taller. He projected that people would reside on the fringes of cities—what we now call suburbs. While trains in America do not exceed speeds of 150 miles per hour, the Chunnel and the Bullet come close. Photographs are indeed

"televised at a distance" through the invention of the satellite. People
have been known to fight with "forts on wheels" through the use of
tanks. With the invention of greenhouses, gardens are "under glass."
Exercise is indeed "compulsory" in public schools. All of these were
predicted by Watkins.

Some of Watkins's predictions were not only met, but have been
greatly surpassed. For instance, a one-pound motor can do far more than
the work of two horses.

Lest one be tempted to advance Watkins's status from predictor to
prophet, I must point out that a few of his predictions failed to pass the
test of time. We still have the letters C, X, and Q in our English alpha-
bet, and automobiles are rarely cheaper than horses. But I believe that
Watkins did amazingly well, even if his predictions then appeared to be
"far out."

Some of the things you will read in this book may seem a little far
out. The church is being forced to rethink its methods in order to appeal
to a new kind of people. New methods always run the risk of appearing
infeasible. New methods, however, do not imply new content. The key
to our future will be casting the "old" gospel in a mold that people in
today's world will view with interest. Enough interest to explore its
contents.

In the year 1900, Watkins tried to think about what a future America
would be like. Around the same time, a Russian literary critic and theo-
logian, Dmitri Merejkowski, thought about the future of his own country.
While Watkins was contemplating what America would be like today,
Merejkowski was contemplating a Russia characterized by freedom of
religion. The surprise tumbling of the Berlin Wall allows us to test
Merejkowski's predictions. Judge the accuracy of the predictions for
yourself as the following words reveal his thoughts almost a century ago:

> The Russian communists, petty devils, . . . are at this moment
> serving Christ as no one has served Him for a long time. The most
> needful thing for the Gospel is to wipe away the dust of the ages—
> familiarity—to make it new, as though written yesterday, to make it
> "dread," "wondrous," as it has not been since early Christian days.
> And this the Russian communists are doing most adequately by
> trying to alienate people from it, forbidding it, seeking to destroy it.
> If only they knew what they were doing! But they will not know till

their end comes. . . . No: man will not forget the Gospel. He will remember, he will read with such eyes, such dread, such wonder, as we cannot picture. Nor can we picture the passionate outburst of love for Christ which will ensue. Has there been such an outburst since He lived on earth? Perhaps Russia will begin that outburst which will become world-wide.[2]

For a very long time, Russian religion and politics were mutually exclusive. Throughout most of this century, religion was indeed kept behind closed doors in Russia. Andrew Greeley writes:

If one wanted to get ahead in Russian society, one either professed atheism and stayed away from churches or kept one's religious propensities a secret. Seminaries were closed, churches turned into museums . . . the clergy were rigidly controlled.

Greeley also reports that nine out of ten Russians were not raised in church and three out of four, at one time, did not believe in God. "Never before in human history has there been such a concerted effort to stamp out not merely a religion, but all trace of religion."[3]

What about today? We all know that Russia is experiencing freedom of religion for the first time in this century. But just how accurate was Merejkowski in his predictions? Very accurate. Today it seems that Russia has been given a gift. A gift of seeing the gospel with untainted vision. A gift of realizing a revelation from long ago. That gift has enabled the work of Christ to grow to new heights in that country. Greeley attributes Russia's resurgence in religion to its repression of religion in past decades. Just what Merejkowski predicted. Based upon "the only data currently available at the present time to scholars around the world about religion in Russia . . . God seems to be alive and well and living in all Russia."[4] Today, three-quarters of the Russians believe in God. A fifth of all Russians have shifted from being atheists to theists in a dramatically short period of time.[5]

Analyzing the Present

It would be wonderful if American churches could receive the same gift as Russian churches, the gift of discovering Christ anew. But with at least 28 percent of Americans owning five or more Bibles, that may not be possible. American churches might, however, have a more realistic opportunity, one still related to Merejkowski's dream for the world. The greatest gift for American churches might be the converse of what is happening in Russia. For a country inundated with Bibles, it may be impossible to view the gospel with a virgin sense of wonder. Even though American churches do not have the luxury of coming to the gospel for the first time in seventy years, they are faced with the task of appealing to a world they have not really viewed for a long time. Rather than viewing the gospel with new eyes, the goal for American churches should be to view the rest of the world with new eyes.

The world has changed right before our eyes, and many American Christians have failed to see the changes. To many, that is very bad news. But isn't God in the business of bringing good news out of bad? God just may be able to turn the American churches' lack of appeal to the people around them into something wonderful!

Sometimes someone or some country must wander far off before it can return to its original task. Like the story of the Prodigal Son. The younger returns ready for new heights of service. The older appears destined for a life of mediocrity, suffering from lukewarm love. Russia had wandered far away from the gospel. Parts of America have lost the vision for their homeland mission field. Those distances may eventually renew both countries.

Witnessing to a brand new world around us might even prompt us to see a new Jesus from within the church. Yes, maybe someday, Merejkowski's vision will be fully realized throughout the world.

The goal for American churches should be to take the gospel of Jesus Christ to people who have never heard such a name. There are such people right here in America. If the churches can discover how to do this, they will again come alive. They will awaken. What would a church look like that accomplished this task? Due to increasing complexities and diversities within our society, it may not be recognizable as a church by today's standards. But if it finds a way to bring the gospel to people in the world and helps them grow in their understanding of the

Lord to a point where the new converts also begin to meet the needs of others, then, by definition, it will still be a church, no matter how different it looks.

As exciting as it is to predict the future, I must confess that this book is far more a look into the church today than it is a look into the future. That's okay. Telling it like it is has its own merit. Telling it like it is was actually as important a job for biblical prophesiers as telling the future, and it is as important to my own preaching and teaching as the fulfillment of biblical prophesies. But, like Watkins and Merejkowski, I will not be able to resist trying to predict some of the things that might happen to the church in the future. Not with the accuracy of a prophet, but, I hope, with the care of a priest.

This book is about megatrends in the church. Taken together, the seven megatrends form a snapshot of today's church. For a few of the megatrends, there is enough evidence to suggest that we are well into "the new." For others, there is barely enough evidence to label the emerging pattern a megatrend—and yet I do take that leap. Tomorrow's church may not embrace all seven new megatrends. I firmly believe, however, that tomorrow's church will imitate none of the seven old patterns. Churches may not incorporate the precise principles described in this book, but they will be forced to change their approaches toward evangelism, discipleship, programming, and so forth, in some fashion, due to the shift that is taking place.

Change is sweeping across our American churches. This book seeks to collect the particles of some of those changes, even before the dust fully clears. An obvious question to ponder is—what stirred up the dust in the first place? Did something prompt the changes occurring in the church today? What caused seven aspects of the church to change so dramatically? Did anything precipitate the megatrends? The answer? A paradigm shift generated the megatrends. The order went something like this:

- A paradigm began to shift.
- Due to the paradigm shift, the church began to recognize that many of the old methods aimed at accomplishing traditional church tasks were no longer working.
- The church tried new methods of accomplishing its age-old purposes.

- Principles underlying notable new methods emerged.
- Underlying principles = megatrends.

Somewhere along the way a paradigm shift began to incite many other changes in the church. Before we can talk of shifting paradigms, however, we must know what a paradigm is.

Paradigms

Chances are, you have already heard the word paradigm. It has become the buzzword of the nineties. John Huey writes, "How a word as obscure and awkward as paradigm has fallen into common usage among executives is difficult to fathom, but it has become truly the buzzword of the age."[6] The following discussion begins to describe the business of paradigms—a business that has become a captivating sensation.

What Is a Paradigm?

A paradigm is a way of viewing the workings of a system. It is a method of sense making. A paradigm involves all of the ways that a group chooses to make sense about issues. So paradigms involve boundaries. Groups maintain both acceptable and unacceptable methods of interpretation. The grouping of acceptable forms of interpretations comprise a paradigm. A paradigm is the integration of all of the "givens" or assumptions people make about issues.

The word paradigm was a Latin word originally meaning "pattern." It was introduced into the mainstream by Thomas Kuhn, now a professor emeritus at MIT. "Kuhn used paradigm to describe archetypal scientific constructs—like Newton's laws of physics—that define the way other scientists come to look at the world."[7] Joel Barker, a former English teacher, is given credit for popularizing the term. Barker is one of the most demanded speakers in the business world today, often called upon to describe the business of paradigms to groups of executives.

What Is a Paradigm Shift?

If a paradigm involves a set of assumptions, then a paradigm shift is defined by a dramatic alteration in the set of assumptions held by a particular individual or group.

Many have suggested that our entire American society has experienced a paradigm shift. John Naisbitt talks of societal megatrends that emerge from the bottom up. He was among the first to talk about the impact of becoming an information society rather than a society that depends solely upon industry for its economy.[8] Alvin Toffler refers to this societal shifting as the third wave of society:

> A new civilization is emerging in our lives. . . . This new civilization brings with it new family styles; changed ways of working, loving, and living. . . . Millions are already attuning their lives to the rhythms of tomorrow. . . . The dawn of this new civilization is the single most explosive fact of our lifetimes.[9]

In addition to society, many organizations have experienced paradigm shifts in recent years. People do not feel the same way toward a variety of institutions as they used to. The larger societal paradigm shift appears to have affected schools, hospitals, colleges, and service clubs. The church is not alone in its experiences of change.

What Is a Paradigm Shifter?

"A paradigm shifter is someone who throws out the rules of the game and institutes radical, not incremental, change— a leader who foments revolution, not evolution."[10] Many people have agreed that paradigm shifters often come from the "outside." Those most likely to bring about radical change are those who are unfamiliar with the organization in the first place.

The message here is that people who are already very familiar with the church need to talk to people who are not. Today's church has a great need to discover what unchurched people perceive to be barriers to faith and worship. Tomorrow's church will learn as much from outsiders as from insiders.

Steven Covey writes, "The most significant breakthroughs have been breaks with old ways of thinking, the old models and paradigms."[11] The church desperately needs help in developing breakthroughs that break with old ways of thinking. Old ways that simply do not reach or help people anymore.

What Is a Congregational Paradigm Shift?

A current paradigm shift in our society is prompting a paradigm shift within the church. Van der Brent states, "The fact that a basic paradigm shift is taking place is by no means a tentative theory or mere supposition . . . renewal cannot come simply by rethinking aims and functions and by rearranging programmes."[12] As Van der Brent suggests, a paradigm shift involves the adoption of a whole new set of assumptions.

The church today appears to be at a watershed moment in history. Shawchuck and Perry explain, "The environment of every church can best be described as turbulent . . . gone (perhaps forever) are the quiet pastoral days when environmental changes come slowly and predictably."[13] Warner asserts, "The sociology of American religion is undergoing a period of ferment, interpreted herein as a paradigm shift in process."[14]

What assumptions are changing in the church? Three are worth noting here and will be detailed further in the next chapter. First, many churches have begun operating as if they were relating to an indifferent or even hostile society, breaking a previously held assumption of societal respect and admiration. A second given in the church involved defining success by numerical growth. Today when a church defines success by some other means, it has altered a pivotal rule. The third assumption being challenged located the enemy of the church in the personality of Satan and nowhere else. Today many leaders on the left and right fringes of the church have demonized the opposition, formerly accepted as a brother or sister in Christ. When people within the church began to challenge these three assumptions regarding the church, a paradigm shift began to materialize. The roots of every megatrend presented in this book can be traced to one of these three factors that have given rise to a paradigm shift in our churches.

This book is about the changes taking place in churches. Small churches. Large churches. Rural churches. City churches. I have not talked to one pastor who has not experienced some sense of a major transformation in his or her congregation. Pastors feel a new church beginning to emerge from under their feet.

Why Church Leaders Have Kept the Paradigm Shift a Secret

These changes did not come overnight. For roughly thirty years the church has been experiencing major change. The purpose of this book is to bring some of those changes to the surface. It is my conviction that many pastors have recognized that their churches are changing in a dramatic way. They have begun to lead and operate differently. Most, however, haven't told their membership why.

There could be many reasons for this. Let me suggest a few. Once you announce you are shifting toward a new way of doing things, you may sense you can no longer go back. Many leaders have made subtle changes in worship, board structures, and committee agenda with a feeling that "if this doesn't work, I can always go back to the old way of doing things." Once you announce your changes, however, you have lost this luxury.

Another reason for this lack of dialogue between pastors and parishioners may be due to the fact that a large part of the change is portrayed as bad news. I believe the changes occurring in churches are related to, but not controlled by, a long-term decline in church membership across the board. The paradigm shift covers something much broader than a need for downsizing. Still, the shift is connected to a decline. When we talk about the shift, we usually get around to talking about the decline as well. So, many times we avoid talking about the shift.

I believe there is also a lack of recognition of the magnitude of the paradigm shift. Those who have read little and talked to others infrequently about the changes they are experiencing are tempted to think that only a few congregations have been affected by such changes. Call it a wave. Call it a storm. Call it a shift. But it's here. When it fully capsizes us, it will probably be bigger than any of us could see with our prophetic telescopes.

Finally, I am pretentious enough to suggest that pastors, pastoral staff, and laity have not openly discussed the changes because an adequate resource for discussing these trends has not yet been written! Adequate or not, this is at least a resource that can provide a framework for such discussion with all types of people.

Whatever the reason may be, it would be unwise for the leadership of the church to change modes and methods for very long without informing the rest of the church body. Let me explain. One of the trends I will discuss in this book is a move to a more lateral style of leadership, as opposed to a vertical style where the leadership makes decisions with little input from others. If this trend is accurate and long lasting, which I believe it is, it is extremely dangerous for the leadership of the church to change its style without informing the membership. Sooner or later, the membership will cry out, "Why didn't you tell us this was going on? We would have liked to help." Some may be not only vocal but also irate.

It is time to let laity in on the secret. It is time for clergy and laity to talk together about the changes occurring in the church. This is a book to be discussed by teams of clergy and laity. If you are a pastor-reader, pass this book along to one of your parishioners. If you are a layperson, pass it along to your pastoral leadership. Better yet, stop reading, and form a study group of laity and pastoral staff from your church and study the book together!

The Paradigm Shift and the Decline

Earlier I alluded to a relationship between the decline in church membership and the changes taking place in our churches. Allow me to provide a few more thoughts about this relationship as I perceive it. I believe the decline in church membership is correlated with the changes taking place in the churches, but I see no direct cause and effect relationship. Many of the changes affecting both church and society are not related to decline in church participation. It is the decline, however, that has signaled the need for change in many churches. In some ways, the decline may be a blessing. Without decline, many churches would never be given the go-ahead to operate differently. The "why fix it if it ain't broke?" attitude has long been a motto of many churches. But this motto doesn't hold water because it assumes that everything is okay as long as you are meeting the needs of the church members you already have. But while the church was proclaiming this slogan, along came a generation that stayed away from the church because the church was not meeting its needs.

Because most churches either declined or were not able to make the subtle changes needed to appeal to this new generation, they are now faced with a major overhaul if they wish to add younger members. Because of the drastic societal paradigm shift, churches are now faced with appealing to a new generation in what appears to be a new society! What a frightening proposition. And what an awe-inspiring moment in church history! The church is so far out on a limb that it can do nothing but pray and ask God to guide the way. There will be no returning, only renewing, revitalizing, and transforming. Send in the megatrends. Let the discussions begin!

CHAPTER TWO

Painting the Big Picture

The subheads in this chapter will set a pattern for each subsequent chapter. As each megatrend stemming from the paradigm shift is revealed in future chapters, I will show where we have been and where we are headed. I will give ample support to show the reason for the change and the need for each trend. Finally, I will challenge congregations to begin discussing and applying the trends.

Due to a paradigm shift, several methods in the church no longer yield prosperous results. Anyone wanting to suggest means for improvement within the church is faced with several options. The person might suggest a variety of new methods to try, presenting the multiplicity of options as a menu from which church members can choose their favorite. As a second option, the person might choose a few favorites and build a case for each one. As a third option, the person might look at several new methods and search for an underlying principle behind the new methods that appear to be working. I have chosen the third option. In short, megatrends = approaches.

For example, the megatrend of relational evangelism, presented in the following chapter, is not a method. It is a principle or approach that might give rise to several evangelistic programs. Immigrant education is not merely a discipleship program. It is a principle underlying an entirely new educational model for the local church that can influence the ways a church trains new members, assimilates people, and implements the Sunday school program. Part 2 of this book will describe each of the seven megatrends.

The big picture must be detailed a bit further, however, before we proceed to our discussion of the individual megatrends. There is a danger in talking about specific aspects of the church independently of one another: One might lose sight of the whole. Every aspect of the church is changing and many of the changes are linked. So before heading to the individual parts, I will present analysis and evidence regarding the changes occurring with respect to the big picture of the church.

Where We've Been

The church is in the midst of a paradigm shift influenced by three main factors. These three main sources are responsible for the spectacular changes occurring in today's churches. The first, and most influential, source relates to a newly defined era for the church, an era characterized most profoundly by a new relationship between church and society. Some have implied that this is the only source of change, but I believe that there are at least two other independent sources compelling today's churches to reshape their identities. The second source of change relates to a redefinition of success caused by the church not having as many people and resources available as in previous years. For the first time in history, mainline churches in America are experiencing decline across the board. The third source of change relates to a need both for identifying with a particular group and polarizing the opposition. As people experience changes, they have a need to feel they are not alone in the changes. Identifying with a group can lead to choosing sides and choosing sides can lead to blaming. Many have sought to blame others for the changes and the declining numbers within the church, making the changes more public.

As you will see, a new era has been the catalyst for the changes, the decline has given the church permission to speak out, and the need for group identification has caused church leaders to speak with a sense of boldness and urgency they otherwise would not have had.

A New Era for the Church

The first source of the changes experienced in today's churches relates to a shift in the relationship between church and society. Many writers have proposed that the church is in a brand new era. An era is not a short period of time. Within one era, a multitude of generations can come and go. Entire nations can be developed, go to war, and fall again several times. Centuries can pass. So when we begin to shift from one era to another, it's a big deal. A very big deal.

Loren Mead suggests that there have been only two eras of the church up until now.[1] He labels them the era of the Apostolic Paradigm and the era of the Christendom Paradigm:

1. The Apostolic Paradigm—(A.D. 30 to 313) characterized in the following ways:
    a. The church began to define itself.
    b. The church sought to evangelize its immediate community.
    c. The church developed clear definitions of who was in the church and who was out.

2. The Christendom Paradigm—(A.D. 313 to 1963) characterized in the following ways:
    a. The boundaries between the church and the state disintegrated.
    b. The boundaries between the church and the community disintegrated.
    c. The administration of the church sent missionaries on behalf of local congregations.
    d. Church communities were divided by geographic boundaries or neighborhoods.
    e. The structure of the church became unified in order for the whole thing to be managed as a unit.
    f. Laity were expected to support the church in all ways.

The current church era is yet to be named.

Paul Dietterich suggests that the church has experienced three eras and is currently seeking to define a fourth.[2] Dietterich divides Mead's second era into two periods. Dietterich's third and fourth eras take a particularly American view of things. He names and characterizes his eras in the following ways:

1. The Early Churches—(A.D. 30 to 311)
    a. The church tried to live by the Beatitudes.
    b. The church held a dislike for the status quo of society.
    c. The church experienced persecution from the community.

     d. People joined the church at great personal risk.

     e. The church developed the spiritual gifts of its members.

2. The Imperial Church—(A.D. 311 to 1789)
   a. Persecution directed at the church ceased.
   b. The persecuted became the persecutors.
   c. Entire communities were labeled as Christian.
   d. The church became a tool of the government.
   e. State churches developed.

3. The Establishment Church—(A.D. 1789 to 1960)
   a. The church grew rapidly.
   b. Mainline denominations grew rapidly.
   c. "Christian" and "American" became synonymous.
   d. Educators and politicians came from churches.
   e. The "haves" gave to the "have-nots."

4 The Post-Establishment Church—(A.D. 1960 to present)
   a. Freedom not to participate in the church emerges.
   b. Science and technology advance.
   c. Religious pluralism develops.
   d. Church shopping develops.
   e. Privatization becomes the norm.

Mead, Dietterich, Hall,[3] and many others explain that today's church is much more like the early church than the church that has dominated the world during most of the years since Christ. Today's church is like the early church in that congregations are seeking to minister to the people in their immediate communities. Today's church must go out into the community to attract people. The days of opening the doors and waiting for the people to enter are long gone because the church has lost the appeal to society it once had. Slice it a hundred different ways, but the dominant aspect of the new era for today's church is the fact that today's society no longer respects the church as it used to.

Society is becoming increasingly hostile toward the church. Remember when Beaver, Wally, June, and Ward all attended church together? When was the last time you saw that on television? Remember when the pastorate was the most respected profession in America? Separation of church and state is a much more volatile topic for today's generation than it was for the previous generation.

It will not get any better because the church's core values and beliefs are no longer held by society. Today's church must begin to set a new standard for what it means to be faithful to God. In previous years, there was only one standard for a church being faithful to God: numerical growth. But let's admit that it was easier to recruit when people did not have to change very much to become church members. Today's church is faced with a new kind of challenge of redefining itself in a malevolent world. What a tremendous opportunity!

Society has changed. The church now finds itself in the precarious position of responding to needs of a changed society. Unless the church is committed to a constant struggle to appeal to the world around it, it will fail in its efforts to be the church in today's world.

Today's church has a mission field at its front door because church and society are no longer synonymous. As you will see in subsequent chapters, this newly defined relationship between church and society is giving rise to a multitude of changes and a variety of megatrends within the church.

A Period of Decline

Every mainline denomination in America has declined in the last thirty years. More than anything else, the decline has given today's church an opportunity to make changes. Many institutions refuse to change until their backs are against the wall. For the institution of the church, that time has come.

But the church cannot afford to respond to decline the way that other institutions and businesses respond to decline. Stephen Warner has suggested that the dominant paradigm for interpreting the sociology of American churches should not be an analysis of the dominant church culture, but rather an analysis of the vital expression of groups within the American church. He uses this concept of groups to show how American churches have traditionally responded to change. There is no Church of America, only churches in America. With no ties to the government, many American churches find themselves at crucial turning points as they seek to increase their market share of the whole.[4] But this could be a dangerous approach, as Dietterich points out:

Church leaders who interpret the current moment in history as decline will become frightened by the losses of members, money, and
influence. . . . They will therefore attempt to reclaim the past by
investing in crash programs to enlist more members, market themselves, build up finances, and improve management.[5]

That kind of strategy will not work because today's churches find
themselves in a whole new environment. Working harder in the same
old ways will not help churches move in the right direction; it will only
get them in the wrong direction faster!
It is not simply a matter of working harder or working faster for
today's churches. Rather, it is a matter of working smarter. George
Orwell, in *Animal Farm*, describes the personality of Boxer, the horse:

Boxer was the admiration of everybody . . . now he seemed more
like three horses than one; there were days when the entire work of
the farm seemed to rest on his mighty shoulders.

Later Boxer is faced with a crisis and decides that the correct response is
to work even harder. Orwell says, "His answer to every problem, every
setback, was 'I will work harder!'—which he had adopted as his personal motto."[6]
Churches today must view the decline as a wake-up call— not to
work harder, but to redefine the very core of what it means to be a
church! The decline is forging the church toward a new definition of
success, a new definition of what it means to be faithful.

Group Identification

A third source of the changes in today's churches stems from a height-
ened awareness of our differences. At a time when the society has become more pluralistic, the church has become more aware of its differences. Some have used these differences to suggest that if others were
more like them, things would not be so bad. I have heard liberals blame
conservatives for the decline in church membership, and I have heard
conservatives blame liberals. I have heard people cite the lack of prayer
in schools as a reason for the decline, and I have heard others cite the
lack of tolerance as the reason.

The reason for all the finger pointing is simple. In a time of transition, everyone wants a little company. Everybody wants to be on a winning team. When people experience change, it can appear that there are sides to be chosen and a victory to be won. Sides of past and future, left and right, good and evil. Choosing sides paints the picture in black and white rather than shades of gray. Choosing sides augments the awareness of both the changes occurring and the differences experienced. The need for group identification has made uniqueness a source of contention rather than a cause for celebration. In the biblical story of the rich man and Lazarus, the rich man had drawn a circle tightly around his riches. Following his death, he found himself on the wrong side of the line. Many today fear being on the wrong side of the line in the moment of death.

The early church sought clear definitions of who was in and who was out. We are returning to that phenomenon once again. People are starting to define who should be in the church and who should be out of the church based upon doctrinal views, biblical interpretations, and other litmus tests. Problems occur when you draw the boundaries of your "in circle" differently than I draw mine.

Some draw very narrow circles. Let me give you an example. In my small association of six churches, I was the only pastor who did not get a personal letter of invitation to a new conservative pastors' fellowship group. I was informed that during the first two meetings, one could sense an air of camaraderie and fellowship. During their third meeting, however, they began to define exactly what it meant to be a conservative pastor. That was the beginning of the group's self-destruction. Apparently some had not drawn the circle narrow enough.

At the other end of the spectrum, some purposely choose to draw very large circles. Some church leaders suggest that today's churches must work together if they are to make a difference in society. Some reach out and include not only all Christian groups, but all faith groups in their circle. Those who have already drawn their circle with a much smaller compass (do they still use those things?) react negatively. They feel no need to be a part of this larger group because they have already identified with a smaller circle.

At times ecumenical inclusion seems to climb to new heights. At other times it seems that churches of different backgrounds or denominations cannot work together within one small rural community. It depends on where the lines have been drawn and by whom. The only constant through all of this is that everyone feels the strong need to be in some circle, whether it be small or large. No one minds succeeding alone, but in an age where failure seems as imminent as success, no one wants to fail alone.

This phenomenon of group identification is not restricted to churches. The person some have termed as the most popular political figure of our day, Rush Limbaugh, makes his living complaining about the work of other people. Part of Limbaugh's appeal lies in recruiting others into what he believes to be the correct movement to guide our nation through its turbulent times. People with no authority seek out others with authority to carry out their circle-drawing activity for them. Those already possessing a little authority constantly recruit more people to increase their authority.

By definition, circle drawing creates two feelings: inclusion and exclusion. At its best, circle drawing provides a sense of belonging. At its worst, it can lead to "witch hunting." Gerald Arbuckle connects the increase in witch hunting today to the dramatic shifts occurring in our churches. He states that whenever people begin to feel that things are not working as they used to, they look for someone to blame. He explains:

> Anthropologically, witch-hunting in modern or traditional cultures has several functions: to explain what cannot be understood, to control the uncontrollable, and to account for the problem of evil personally and in society. . . . We define what does not belong to our group and equivalently call it dirty.[7]

In its mildest form, blaming others for change surfaces as an arrogance about one's own views. In its ugliest form, the blame surfaces as a demonizing of the opposition. Roger Fredrikson recently reported in a conference setting that 117 Southern Baptist pastors are being terminated every month, presumably by discontented congregations blaming the pastors for whatever has "gone wrong." Change causes stress, and stress can create some extremely hurtful situations, not just among Southern Baptists, but in all denominations and faith groups. When someone tries to pick a fight long enough, someone else in the room will eventually respond.

The good side of this news, if there is one, is that there is a logical

reason for the increase in witch hunting. If it were not these issues divid-
ing us, it would surely be another set of issues. It is not so much the
issues themselves that divide us between two poles; let's call them right
and left. Rather, the struggles are merely signs of the times of transition
that seek to divide us between a past and a future; the future being so
different from the past is what forces people to choose between a left and
a right. Arbuckle's theory also suggests that the witch-hunting phenomena may be temporary. *Temporary*, however, is a relative term.

The bad side of Arbuckle's news is that the blaming will probably
continue until we have a better handle on what the church will be like in
the next era. Maybe if we tried to define how things are changing, at
least for this year, or month, or day, it would relieve the stress a bit and
begin to curtail the witch hunting.

I recently watched an episode of "Lassie." (I have always been
amazed at the environment in which little Timmy lives. It is a mountain-
ous region that appears to support both agriculture and mining. I have
also witnessed every form of wild life imaginable on the show.) In this
particular episode, Timmy searches for the animal that destroyed his
mom's strawberry patch. Unknown to Timmy, a wallaby is to blame.
Timmy and one of his friends track the wallaby. When they spot it,
Timmy's friend asks, "What is it?"

Timmy responds, "It looks like a giant rabbit to me."

Later, when the owners of the wallaby appear on the scene, they
allude to the danger involved if Lassie comes near the wallaby.

Timmy's mother responds, "Oh, Lassie wouldn't harm another
animal."

The owner replies, "Oh, it is not the dog I meant. With a wallaby's
powerful tail and sharp claws, it could rip a dog to shreds!"

We often misidentify the enemy and underestimate its nature. Many
church leaders have chosen to blame other church leaders for the un-
pleasant changes they are experiencing. As the church progresses
through this transitional period, we must keep in mind who our enemy
is and who our sisters and brothers in Christ still are. One of the most
powerful uniters in life is a common enemy. In 1 Samuel 23, David and
Saul recognized the Philistines as their common enemy and paused from
their struggle with each other long enough to battle the Philistines.

Today's church finds itself in turbulent waters. Once the storm has
subsided, every church leader would like to look back and point out that

he or she was aboard the ship that most successfully navigated the high seas. Will it be the megachurch? Will it be bivocational ministry? Will it be lay ministry? Will it be the conservatives? Will it be the ecumenists? But let's admit that there may be several passageways into the future. There probably will not be only one form or structure that emerges. I believe that we will live to witness several completely different models for congregational ministry taking shape in the future.

This book will primarily detail the methods, rather than the structures, that are emerging from today's churches. But, a few times throughout the book, I will suggest entirely new structures that churches may incorporate to accomplish their purposes.

Where We're Headed

Loren Mead talks of a once and yet to be discovered future church.[8] Keith Russell advocates embarking upon a search for the church.[9] Envisioning involves seeing as far as you can and then guessing what might lie beyond. Envisioning is always a continuous process because every day you travel a little bit further down the road.

Megatrends

Difficult as it is to see into the future, we ought to at least try to understand what methods or, better yet, broadly based approaches have been helpful to others, rather than proceeding blindly down the road. John Naisbitt and Patricia Aburdene popularized the term megatrends. "Trends," Naisbitt says, "like horses, are easier to ride in the direction they are already going." He adds, "You may decide to buck the trend, but it is still helpful to know it is there."[10] In the eyes of Naisbitt, when a trend begins to reveal a major transformation that is taking place in all of society, it deserves to be called a megatrend.

In this book, I will describe how seven aspects of the church are changing. I have chosen what I believe to be the seven most important aspects of the church. The first four relate to the fundamental purposes of the church: evangelism, discipleship, mission, and spirituality. Into whatever form the next church eventually pours itself, I cannot and will not try to envision a church that does not choose to emphasize these four aspects in some way. We must strip away only the traditions, methods, and ways that are not working, not the mission, the purpose, or the kernels of truth about God.

The next three trends relate to methods in the church: leadership, programming, and planning. I believe that these current shifts are transformational enough to be called congregational megatrends.

Each megatrend is presented as a new approach for one of the objectives of the church. I have chosen approaches that I believe are beneficial for the church. I consistently encourage the church I pastor to move in the direction of the seven megatrends presented in this book. These are not merely "coulds" for me. They are "shoulds."

If I were discussing methods, I would feel uncomfortable promoting just one for, say, evangelism or education. These megatrends, however, are broader than a single method. Several alternate methods may be tried from a single megatrend. I have searched for helpful underlying approaches to the methods I see churches using today. Each approach detailed in this book may not be the megatrend that emerges for tomorrow's churches, but I believe that each new approach is currently more beneficial for the church than the seven old approaches detailed in the "Where We've Been" sections. In part 2, I will portray seven principles as megatrends for the church.

Crossroads

Today's church is faced with an uncertain future. When a future becomes so uncertain, people begin to question the possibility of moving forward at all. Where will the church find the strength to forge ahead? A motto has been attributed to the French Foreign Legion:

> If I falter, push me on.
> If I stumble, pick me up.
> If I retreat, shoot me.[11]

I have a sense that many churches have traveled so far down a new road that it would be virtually impossible for them to retreat to the place where they forged a new trail. Yet other churches find themselves still at the crossroads. Lloyd Allen describes the phenomenon of crossroads in one's personal life:

> Three options are open to the believers standing in the center of a spiritual crisis. They can remain where they are, they can turn around and go back, or they can go forward. Two of these choices are dead ends and the third is full of danger.[12]

It is the same with the church today. We want to hold onto something old and familiar that we can feel every now and then and know everything is still okay, like Lennie from the book *Of Mice and Men*:

> "What'd you take outa that pocket?"
> "Ain't a thing in my pocket," Lennie said cleverly.
> . . . "You got it in your hand."
> "I ain't got nothin', George. Honest."
> "Give it here!" said George.
> . . . Lennie's closed hand slowly obeyed. George took the mouse and threw it across the pool to the other side, among the brush. "What you want of a dead mouse, anyways?"[13]

Many churches would still like to be about the business of mice and men, of trivial arguments and hierarchical control, of old ways and traditions, rather than about change and openness. We'd like to hold something in our pocket—even if it's dead—to remind us of the glory days of our church. The old ways that we hold onto may have died in value long ago. Still we hold them dear, confusing the vessel with its contents, the wineskins with the wine. Transformational change will not come easily for the church.

The church is changing. The change is significant enough to be termed a crisis. The word crisis stems from a Latin root which means "to part" or "to separate."[14] The church is currently faced with parting from the old ways of doing things. The church must orient itself toward the future. The word orient originally meant the direction of the rising sun.[15] Many believe that the sun is setting on the church. Rather, it may be that the church has been in a period of darkness, and a totally new sun is just about to emerge upon the horizon. To follow that sun, the church must venture out. "Old ways die hard. . . . It is more peaceful to stay in one's

office than to venture out into the world. It is more secure in a committee meeting than it is in the world."[16] The church has always been directed "out" but usually felt more comfortable "in." The outside world is
not as friendly as it used to be, but now, more than ever, it needs to be
the church's focal point.

Belling the Cat

We would have all been better off if someone would have belled the cat
long before now. We have waited too long to announce to the congregations that change in the church is inevitable.

> When people must act individually and hope that the momentum
> will build up, the question arises, "Who is going to be first?" Such a
> leader will pay a very high cost—possibly his life. . . . Most find the
> costs exceed the benefits.[17]

The church made subtle changes for many years, seeking to adapt to
societal changes. With the advent of the paradigm shift in the church has
come a recognition of the need for a complete overhaul. We didn't overhaul earlier because the potential punishments outweighed the potential
rewards. After decades of decline, that has changed.

The megatrends presented in this book will not sound entirely new.
Some terms may sound new, others quite familiar. All of the megatrends
ought to at least make sense and feel right—or I've missed the target in
that area. Keep in mind that the megatrends are intended to portray
broad principles underlying the new approaches to traditional church
purposes. This book is about belling the megatrends in our churches.
Church leaders must inform the rest of the church that it will not be business as usual in the coming years. This book gives the reasons why. The
time has come to tell the church that it must become a new church if it is
going to survive.

Up to this point, I have described some of the broad changes that
have touched American congregations. I now will offer support to show
the basis upon which many of these insights were formed. The support
will be presented in four sections: statistical, theoretical, anecdotal, and
theological.

Statistical Support

Yes, churches are declining. Originally researchers thought the decline
started in the year 1965. They now believe that growth was dramatically slowing in the 1950s.[18] Based upon a meta-analysis of church
growth and decline studies, Roozen makes the following conclusions:

- Total church attendance and membership are declining.
- The growth rate of all Protestant denominations slowed during the
  1950s.
- In the early 1960s, moderate and liberal Protestant groups actually
  started to lose more members than they gained each year. Today
  that is still the case, although they are not declining as fast today as
  they did in the 1960s.
- Even now, conservative Protestant groups add more than they lose
  each year, although with each passing year, their net gains are getting smaller and smaller.
- The pentecostal/holiness surge in growth slowed dramatically in the
  1980s.
- In terms of membership growth rates, Roman Catholics are leading
  the way in the 1990s.[19]

The above conclusions are not great, but they may appear to be better news than you would have expected. Hold on. Please do not start
celebrating yet. Any good news contained in the above statements is
lessened when several additional factors are added. The first is a meas-
ure of religious climate. Religious climate is an indicator of the importance of religion in one's life. Roozen points out that the overall religious climate, as measured by the *Princeton Index*, has declined about
twice as much as church membership since 1950.[20] In other words, even
those who have not formally severed ties with the church are placing
less importance upon religion in their lives.

A second factor that adds to the bad news is that since the 1950s,
the number of *potential* church members in the United States has actually increased rather than decreased. Mead points out in his book
Transforming Congregations for the Future that the declines in the
Episcopal, Evangelical Lutheran, Presbyterian, United Methodist, and
United Church of Christ denominations would even be worse if they
were reported against U.S. population trends.[21]

A third factor that stirs up more bad news for existing churches is related to church planting. In denominations that are growing, a major reason for growth is often related to new church development and not merely growth in existing churches.[22]

Finally, there is the fact that growing churches are usually in growing areas. Churches that are not in growing areas are fighting a huge uphill battle to grow numerically.

> Although we may hope to reverse that trend and work hard against it, it is clear that very large societal forces are at play, forces over which the evangelism committee of a local congregation has limited power. . . . most congregations will experience the power of the trends the researchers describe. . . . It is just as probable that congregational membership . . . will match the membership declines in the general population, no matter what church leaders do.[23]

All of the above findings point out that the majority of congregations in the United States are in a state of decline rather than a state of growth. That is a very different phenomenon than what the last generation of people in American churches experienced.

Here I want to reinforce a point made earlier. Yes, churches have declined in attendance and membership. This book, however, is not being written because churches are declining. This book is being written because the people in the churches and in society have changed. People are different. Their needs, their hopes, their neighbors, and their friends are different. Recognition of the decline will allow churches to respond to the changes that already have occurred in people.

Theoretical Support

Okay. I now believe that the church has been in a period of decline for several years. But why?

In a lecture at Christian Theological Seminary, Kennon Callahan cited several reasons for the decline of American churches. Three of his reasons, which I paraphrase here, are particularly revealing:

1. A decline in social conformity. People just do not enjoy participating in institutional life the way they once did. This generation is not

as quick to join clubs, service organizations, sororities, or churches as previous generations. Like it or not, peer pressure at one time had a lot to do with people joining churches. At one time, it was "in" to be a church member. Today, in many communities, it no longer is.

2. An increase in freedom of choice. People have more options than they used to have. This includes options for meeting one's spiritual needs. People are choosing means other than corporate worship to meet their spiritual needs.

3. The church's failure to address the changing needs of society. For example, some churches still hold an 11:00 a.m. worship service as the only opportunity for members to worship; they do this without seeking to discover if this is the time at which their members most want to worship Committee and board meetings are seldom adjusted to the needs of all people. Many churches have failed to address the needs of people in closest proximity to their buildings.

In many ways, churches have declined because they have perpetuated old customs. Cueni exhorts,

> "Why?" is the most important question that church leaders can ask: "Why should we do this particular ministry task?" Failure to answer that question in a valid, biblical way wastes tons of leadership energy. Programmatic ships that should never have been built sail out of the harbor for meaningless cruises.[24]

People often complain about the aloofness of government. Bloom suggests that both government and the church have been characterized by a form of self-centeredness. Many people perceive politicians to be more interested in their own pensions and platforms than those of society. Many people also perceive church members to be more interested in meeting one another's needs than of meeting the needs of society. "Religion and national origin have almost no noticeable effect on [people's] social life or their career prospects."[25] Many people believe that today's church is having little affect on this generation or the next.

There are ample theories describing the reasons for the decline in church membership. There are just as many theories suggesting a need for change in the church. Nearly every religious thinker believes that the church of the future must change because the society surrounding the church has changed.[26] "Statistical research, analyses of this culture, and

long-range projections all clearly indicate that ours is no longer a
churched culture."[27] The most often cited need is for the church to look
"out" beyond itself. Many writers suggest that the only real future of the
church lies in its reaching out to its immediate community. Wheatley
agrees that tomorrow's church should reach out more to its community
and suggests that such a task will involve a complete reorientation within
the church. She writes,

> We need courage to let go of the old world, to relinquish most of
> what we have cherished, to abandon . . . what does and doesn't
> work. As Einstein is often quoted as saying, "No problem can be
> solved from the same consciousness that created it. We must learn to
> see the world anew."[28]

Writers in every Catholic and Protestant tradition have harmonized
in their plea for tomorrow's church to reach out. Lutherans, Episcopa-
lians, Methodists, and Catholics have all sung the same song. Fr. Patrick
Brennan, coordinator of the Center for Evangelization, Catechesis, and
Religious Education for Loyola University Institute of Pastoral Studies,
says, "There'll be two churches in the future, a dwindling church with an
aging dying structure and a mission church reaching out to people."[29]

Anecdotal Support

Had enough statistics and theories for now? Let's hear from some real
people about how their lives have been changing. As much as I love
statistics (I really do, I even teach statistics), I have always paid more
attention to people than to numbers. The numbers suggest that changes
are occurring, but, more important, people tell me that churches must
change in order to meet their needs. As I conducted research for this
book, the librarian remarked about the combination of books I was
checking out. That led to a conversation.

She said, "Why can't churches have a Tuesday night service? I
could come then. I can't come on Sunday, or at least not when they meet
on Sunday. Put that in your book, will you?"

I went on to ask her what she would like a Tuesday evening worship
service to do for her.

She replied, "Connect with my life, my friends, my hopes. . . . I would like for it to help me make sense of things."

She is not alone. There are many people who have a longing for God, but no way to fulfill that longing through what today's churches are offering.

Cueni gives an example of a pastor who complains about not being appreciated by his congregation. The pastor laments,

> I cannot understand it . . . I am the best preacher this congregation has had since Dr. . . . The Christian Education program has been acclaimed for excellence in two professional journals. . . . My skills in programming, preaching, and administration are outstanding. Yet, the members of this church don't appreciate me.[30]

Cueni attributes the pastor's sense of being unappreciated to a congregation that ranks ministerial style and personality above competence. I sense a different problem. The pastor in this example may have the right skills for the wrong era! As churches seek to minister outside their walls, they are going to need leaders who can lead them in that direction. Not all seminaries (and I believe I am being polite here) are training pastors to be able to minister to the society and community outside the church.

What will it take to minister to and attract people from today's society? It will take an uncompromising commitment to God. Even though society persecuted the early church, the society still marveled at the Christians' commitment to God. This commitment allowed the early church to grow even in the face of eminent danger on the part of its new members. For today's church to attract people from today's society, people within society must begin to see a clear difference between the people of God and the people of the world. That difference was no more evident in the early church than in the life of Polycarp:

> So, on the day of preparation, mounted police with their usual arms set out about supper-time, taking with them the servant, hurrying "as against a thief." . . . He could have gone away to another farm, but he would not, saying, "The will of God be done." . . . There was so much ado about the arrest of such an old man. . . . Now, as he was entering the stadium, there came to Polycarp a voice from heaven, "Be strong, Polycarp, and play the man." . . . The proconsul urged

him and said, "Swear and I will release thee; curse the Christ." And
Polycarp said, "Eighty and six years have I served him, and he hath
done me no wrong; how then can I blaspheme my king who saved
me?" . . . Then said the Proconsul, "I have wild beasts; if thou repent
not, I will throw thee to them." . . . And Polycarp answered, "Why
delayest thou? Bring what thou wilt." . . . And now things happened
with such speed, . . . for the mob straitway brought together timber
and faggots . . . they were about to nail him to the stake, when he
said, "Let me be as I am. He that granted me to endure the fire will
grant me also to remain at the pyre unmoved without being secured
with nails." . . . The fire took the shape of . . . a ship's sail bellying
the wind, and it made a wall round the martyr's body; like a loaf
being baked or like gold and silver being tried in the furnace . . . and
all the multitude marvelled at the great distance between the unbe-
lievers and the elect.[31]

Few would be willing to make such a statement as Polycarp if it involved
such consequences! But the message is clear. We must find a way to
entice the world by our love for one another, our love for them, and our
uncompromising commitment to God.

Theological Support

Many of today's churches appear to be in a wilderness time. Sound
rough? It need not be so. Wilderness is not all bad. Let me explain. God
delivered the Israelite people of the Old Testament out of slavery and
into the wilderness. So the wilderness must be better than slavery and
oppression! Granted, many of the people at times complained that they
would have been better off in the graves of Egypt than in the wilderness.
    But just what did the Israelites experience in the wilderness? God
cared for their every need. God delivered manna to them from heaven,
water from a rock, and guided them to streams in the desert. God met
every physical need so they might recognize their great spiritual need.
Eventually the Hebrew people began to take advantage of their surroundings and learned to discover God in the wilderness.
    Even though we find ourselves in a wilderness time, churches can
trust that God will continue to meet their needs as they seek out new

ways in which to minister to the people of their communities. I do not believe that the church has outlived its usefulness. In its present structure, it may have. But I believe the people of God will continue to find new ways to evangelize, disciple, grow spiritually, and meet the needs of others. And the church, in whatever form it takes, will continue to be the primary arena for getting those things done.

Epilogue

Nearly every church will eventually be affected by the changes taking place and the patterns that eventually emerge. Hans Kung writes, "Where the available rules and methods fail, they lead the search for new ones."[32] The church will never give up its passion for evangelism, missions, and discipleship; when the old methods for accomplishing those tasks fail, the church will scurry to replace the old methods with new ones.

As I've said, I present the megatrends in the following chapters for the sole purpose of prompting further dialogue and analysis by each individual church. The trends are not meant to be the final word. They are not even meant to be a word accompanied by an exclamation mark. They are based on a belief that the church is in the midst of a paradigm shift that has prompted the need for better approaches. The seven megatrends help us take a look at seven aspects of the church. The seven views have been snapped with my personal camera. Keep in mind that they are one person's assessment of how the church is changing and should change. They will have merit only to the extent that they are examined and recast by others. Following your perusal of these pictures from my angle, get out your own camera and find your own angle.

Where We Begin

Discussing the Trend

1. In what specific ways have you experienced society not being as respectful of your church or other churches as it once was?
2. Discuss the concept of church eras. Is this news? Does it make sense?
3. Has your church grown or declined in the last thirty years? More or less than your community? More or less than your denomination?
4. Recall the "mouse story." What one thing from the past glory days of the church would you like to hold on to?
5. In adopting new innovations, organizations often follow a bell-shaped curve. A few churches will seek to embrace the characteristics as early adopters. Many others will (seemingly all at once) adopt the characteristics of the new change only after witnessing the success of other churches. Other organizations resist change until they find that they can no longer relate to their old environment or no longer find the parts to perpetuate their old mechanisms. Still others slowly decompose. What is your church's history? Are you an early adopter of change? Are you one that has to witness many successes of a new idea in other settings prior to your own implementation of it? Discuss how difficult it is to make changes in your congregation.

Applying the Trend

1. Is there an unchurched person in your community whom you could invite to observe one or some of your church activities and tell you what he or she does not understand?
2. Invite one of your denominational leaders to your church to discuss with you the concept of the changing era or paradigm of the church.
3. If you are not already doing so, convene a group to study this book together.

PART 2

Megatrends

CHAPTER THREE

From Mass Evangelism to Relational Evangelism

This is the first of seven chapters that will portray the changes taking place in one of the established tasks of the church. This chapter explores the task of evangelism.

I currently chair the policy statements and resolutions committee for the American Baptist Churches, USA. I'm biased, but I believe our denomination's policy statement on evangelism includes an outstanding definition of evangelism, which I give here so the reader has a clear understanding of how evangelism is being used in this chapter:

> Evangelism is the joyous witness of the People of God to the redeeming love of God urging all to repent and to be reconciled to God and each other through faith in Jesus Christ who lived, died, and was raised from the dead, so that being made new and empowered by the Holy Spirit believers are incorporated as disciples into the church for worship, fellowship, nurture and engagement in God's mission of evangelization and liberation within society and creation, signifying the Kingdom which is present and yet to come.

In my mind, evangelism incorporates every aspect of a process, from the time a person is drawn to Jesus Christ to the time the person begins to witness to others about the Christ who has been accepted. Today many elements of the evangelization process are in transition.

Where We've Been

In this century American churches have employed five primary modes of evangelism: crusades, children, programming, visitation, and waiting. The fifth method is by far the most popular. Each one of these five methods views potential church members from a macro rather than a micro perspective. Each one portrays evangelism as an activity directed toward a large body of people.

Though people have always received their salvation from God one by one, the church's focus has not always been on the "one." But we are in the midst of a shift: to individualistic evangelism. The church is changing from mass evangelism to relational evangelism.

Crusades

There was a time when most churches held revivals. During revivals people joined churches by the droves. These "revivals" were first of all "evangelistic crusades" and secondly "revivals." Yet the crusades indeed seemed to revive the spirit and personality of the congregation simply by adding new people to it.

Revival messages delivered by evangelistic preachers often contain little new content that might help the mature Christian to grow. I know. I have attended evangelistic crusades. I have heard Billy Graham preach on television. I have attended the Billy Graham School of Evangelism. I have taken an evangelistic preaching class in seminary The format is the same. The speaker tells those in attendance several different times that they will receive an invitation to walk down the aisle and that many of them will choose to do so. The gospel is presented in several ways, and several people come forward.

But lately not as many come forward as in the past. Many churches have stopped holding revivals or evangelistic crusades geared toward people making salvation or church membership decisions because fewer people are choosing to make those decisions among a crowd of strangers.

The church is no longer the social center for a community. Announcing "The church is having special services this week," may once have been a community opportunity for gathering. Now there are so many options vying for time, a crusade at the church isn't even seen as

an option. It may even be seen with derision. In 1991 an auto-mainte-
nance firm in a major metropolitan area showed a man in out-of-date
black and white clothes—obviously a clergyman—commanding a field
of broken and dilapidated cars to "Be healed." The mockery seemed
evident, but at least someone thought it would attract business. So much
for religious experiences being held in high esteem.

Today few churches hold evangelistic crusades geared at either
community or family members. Yet many churches have not replaced
what was once an effective evangelistic strategy with a new one that
works.

Children

Many churches can no longer depend on church families to replenish
their congregations by encouraging children in church families to join the
church. Families are smaller, and fewer children are choosing the same
denomination or church as their parents. I used to say, "The youth are
the future of this church." Then I changed it to, "The youth are the future of somebody else's church." Now even that statement is not true!
We seem to have lost a generation of youth.

Programming

Many churches have falsely perceived their programming as an evangelistic arm of their church. Programs related to music, Bible study, sports,
and fellowship can all add people, but only to the extent that the people
already involved in the programs invite people who are not involved to
participate. Then it becomes evangelistic. Most of the time, that doesn't
happen. Roozen and Hadaway point out that churches that seek to develop their programming as a method of church growth usually do not
succeed, unless this effort is also coupled with intentional evangelistic
efforts.[1]

Visitation

The fourth primary method of twentieth-century evangelism has been
"door-to-door." How, one might ask, can you say that door-to-door
evangelism is mass evangelism? After all, you only knock on one door
at a time. That's true, but the focus is still on the general population, not
the individual. Door-to-door evangelism is mass evangelism if no prior
relationship has been established prior to knocking on that door. In my
experience as a pastor, most people dread door-to-door evangelism:
those making the calls and those receiving the calls. Most people reading this book will not be disappointed to hear that this method is fading.
Rebecca Pippert once observed, "Christians and non-Christians have one
thing in common: They both hate evangelism."[2] Door-to-door evangelism is probably one the main reasons why Pippert's statement is true for
so many people.

Waiting

Callahan points out that churches also once practiced evangelism by
waiting for the masses to come to them. He once said in a conference
that today's churches are waiting for (1) the next wave of immigrants to
come, (2) the next wave of rural people to move to the suburbs, (3) the
next great idea to come from the suburban church model.

In many ways the church is waiting for a savior to resurrect their
evangelism efforts. I t will not happen.

Churches usually combine waiting with friendliness, thinking the
"friendly church" reputation will draw newcomers. Callahan points out
the logical fallacy in this strategy:

> By definition, virtually all churches are friendly churches. By de-
> finition, the only people who are not in a given church are the people
> who did not find that church friendly. Obviously, the people who
> did not find that church friendly, departed quickly.[3]

That is to say that all churches perceive themselves to be friendly.
The better question becomes, "How attractive are we as a congregation
to visitors?"

Even for a church that does an excellent job of welcoming strangers, this method still brings up the same problem faced by evangelistic crusades today: People must have a reason to visit your congregation in the first place.

Other congregations combine waiting with building, believing that if they build it, the people will come. It works in dreams. Rarely in churches. An ancient Chinese proverb says, "A man can stand for long time with his mouth open before a roast duck flies in."

Mass evangelism focuses on the general population. Relational evangelism focuses on the individual. Relationships—not crusades, not programs, not door-to-door visits—are becoming the basis for evangelism. Evangelism is up to us. The day of appealing to the masses is over. The day of friendships has arrived. We will now explore this idea in more detail.

Where We're Headed

Defining Relational Evangelism

Relational evangelism involves sharing the good news about Jesus Christ to someone you already care about and to whom you have already demonstrated God's love in hopes that the one evangelized will do the same. There was a time when many people shared the good news of Jesus Christ with total strangers. Others, who did not possess the gift of evangelism, depended upon these people to make the church grow.

Today it seems we must earn the right to share the good news of Jesus Christ with someone. We must have shared lots of good news with someone before we can talk about the Good News. In a culture concerned with issues of privacy and leery of strangers, we must earn the right to talk to a person about his or her soul. People will no longer cross the threshold of the church building to hear about Jesus without a personal invitation from someone they trust.

There are several contrasts between mass evangelism and relational evangelism:

Mass Evangelism	**Relational Evangelism**
Takes place primarily outside the church	Takes place primarily inside the church
Is done by the pastor	Is done by the laity
Takes place at designated times	Takes place spontaneously
Occurs in an instant	Occurs over time
Appeals to a common denominator	Appeals to each person uniquely

Relational evangelism is not new. Churches have often encouraged members to invite their friends and families to church. But I sense that many church members have viewed relational evangelism as a supplemental activity to the rest of the evangelism efforts of the church. This is what's new: It is no longer supplemental. It has become the primary way that people come to know Jesus Christ.

Relational evangelism involves loving other people. Due to the high level of skepticism toward the church, many people first must be genuinely loved by the church before they can genuinely hear the gospel. We must genuinely love other people before they will be able to hear the gospel in a genuine way. "Committed Christians who do not genuinely love and care for people will be handicapped when it comes to witnessing for Christ in the world."[4] Most people share their love of God with others because they personally know what God has meant to them, and they want others to experience that same sense of joy and peace that only Christ gives. But people are skeptical. They do not readily understand the concept of something for nothing. They do not understand it until the concept has been demonstrated to them by someone they respect.

> In order for the church to reach the grass roots and the unchurched, we need people with more compassion, not more commitment. . . . The text does not say, "We are committed to Jesus because Jesus was first committed to us." It reads, "We love Jesus because Jesus first loved us."[5]

Creating a Climate for Relational Evangelism

Relational evangelism begins with a demonstration of God's love to others. The pastoral leadership should lead the way in reaching out to others. Pastors must lead the way in caring for people, both in the church and in the community. Relational evangelism can be introduced by the pastoral leadership of the church setting a tone for friendships and honest, caring relationships. I believe that a pastor can do more to foster evangelism in a church by promoting a warm and caring attitude and making it clear that every person who visits the church will be accepted for who he or she is, than by detailing numerous accounts of witnessing.

> New leaders must be relational. Relationships are more important than ever. Churches want leaders who are real and approachable. This does not mean they must be extroverts or always working the crowd. Leaders must live where their people live, feel their emotions, and intuitively sense their thoughts.[6]

Taking the Initiative

But relational evangelism does not end with the encouragement of relational leaders, lest we end up with the old "waiting game" approach of evangelism. Church members must also take the initiative of demonstrating their love toward others in the community. Demonstrating one's love toward others as a Christian involves sharing the good news of Jesus Christ, but it may not be necessary to perform this task in a traditional way.

Sharing the good news of Jesus Christ does not have to involve a formal presentation of the gospel. It may be as simple as inviting a friend to church with you and offering to pick a friend up, accompanying you to a special service held by your congregation. Not everyone can share the contents of the gospel in an easy manner. But everyone who is reading this has extended at least one invitation in his life. Think of all the people you have invited to a birthday party, a sorority meeting, a Rotary meeting, a family reunion, or a Tupperware party. Consider giving another invitation to those same people, an invitation to deepen their relationship with Jesus Christ.

Relational Evangelism Is a Process

Evangelism is a process. A seed is planted, watered, cultivated, and eventually harvested. Because evangelistic decisions are most often made public inside the church, and in most cases at the close of a worship service, we might be tempted to conclude that all harvesting takes place as a result of a sermon. Such a view still focuses on mass evangelism as opposed to relational evangelism.

During my pastoral ministry, many people have made public professions of Jesus Christ at the close of a worship service. An extremely small percentage of these instances, however, were actually surprises. In the vast majority of cases, I am aware that a person has already made a choice to accept and follow Jesus Christ and merely has chosen to make the decision public during a worship service. So when did the harvest occur? In most cases, at a time prior to the worship service.

Whatever occurs inside the church to enhance the process of evangelism should be approached from a relational standpoint. What does an individual need to bring a planted evangelistic seed to harvest? Encouragement, support, answers, a safe space in which to ask questions, challenge, dissonance, and love may all be needed in the lives of individual people seeking to know Jesus Christ. Preaching can meet many of an inquirer's needs, but preaching should not be viewed as the sole provider. Classes for the inquirer, opportunities to make friends, places to serve, and chances to grow may all enhance the evangelization process along with hearing God's word.

Four Levels of Relational Evangelism

Relational evangelism is not a single program. As with each megatrend, it is a principle. It is a comprehensive approach to evangelism from which methods may arise. There are four levels of relational evangelism: (1) helping people who visit your church feel accepted regardless of their background; (2) training those with the gift of evangelism to present the gospel to their friends; (3) encouraging others without the gift of evangelism to talk to their friends about what God means to them; (4) encouraging everyone to invite friends to church where they can hear the gospel presented in some format.

The following four sections will provide detailed instructions on how your congregation can become involved in each of these four levels of relational evangelism.

Helping People Feel Accepted

It will not do any good to bring new people into your church if they do not feel accepted once they arrive. Employ various techniques to discover what barriers currently exist in your church toward outsiders.

1. Ask for word-association responses to the name of your congregation. What comes to mind when people hear the name of your church? Try it with Sunday school classes, committees, and out in the community. What do the responses tell you? What do they reveal about your church's ability to attract visitors? Do the results relate more to the personality, heritage, and tradition of your church or more to the attitudes of your specific members?
2. Take an inventory of the types of people in your church neighborhood. Is there a senior citizen complex nearby? Are there gangs? Is there a day care center? Do all of these groups feel welcome in your church? If any of these groups are not present, it might be because they do not feel welcome.
3. Does the socio-economic status of your church match that of your church's neighborhood? If not, what can you do to make people in your church neighborhood feel welcome?
4. Ask a few people who have visited your church recently if they felt welcome. Try to ask people who have not returned. Remember that those who have returned must have thought it was friendly. Try to gather information about your weaknesses and improve upon them.

Encouraging Those with the Gift of Evangelism

Various authors suggest that 5 to 10 percent of your congregation would feel very comfortable presenting the good news of Jesus Christ with others. Do not neglect these people.

1. Find out who they are by helping all members of your congregation discover their spiritual gifts.[7]

2. Train those with the gift of evangelism.
3. Commission those who have the gift of evangelism on behalf of the other members.
4. Once these people have been commissioned, continue to pray for them regularly and publicly.
5. Encourage these people with the gift of evangelism to form a ministry team or group for support.
6. Update their training periodically.
7. As new members who possess the gift of evangelism are added to your church, commission them and add them to the ministry team.

Encouraging Those without the Gift of Evangelism

Commissioning those with the gift of evangelism does not excuse those for whom evangelism does not come naturally. Does your church pass the offering plate only to those who have the gift of giving? For the other 90 to 95 percent of your congregation, try the following steps during five consecutive worship services:

1. Week 1: Give all congregants one week to think of three people they know whom they believe do not attend church now.
2. Week 2: Ask each congregant to think of at least one way that each of the three people could benefit from a stronger relationship with God.
3. Week 3: Ask each congregant to pray the following prayer for her three people, "Lord, please communicate to these three people and let them know what it would mean to have a relationship with you."
4. Week 4: Ask each congregant to add this to his prayer, "God, if there is any way I can help these people have a stronger relationship with you, let me know."
5. Week 5: Set aside a time to celebrate any joys and blessings that have taken place.

Encouraging Everyone to Invite Friends to Church

The heart of relational evangelism involves encouraging church members to present the good news of Jesus Christ to their friends. No matter how hard you try, a significant portion of your congregation will probably never do that. Do not fret. There is yet one more strategy. It works. Even though many people in your church will vehemently resist presenting the good news of Jesus Christ to a friend, most of them would be willing to invite a friend to church—where someone else could do that for them. Every congregation should consistently encourage all members to invite friends to church. One way to do this is through a Friend Day.

Several other available activities are geared specifically toward encouraging church members to invite their friends to church. Consider Bring a Friend Day(s), open houses, house parties, special celebrations of particular occupations within your community, and special concerts or theme worship services throughout the year. Contact your judicatory office, The Alban Institute, or various parachurch groups for more help in implementing any of these ideas.

Statistical Support

Peter Wagner reports that the average Christian church in America can expect at most 10 percent of its membership to have the gift of being an evangelist.[8] That seems to indicate that more people would be willing to invite a friend to church or simply talk about God to a friend than would be willing to conduct door-to-door evangelism or counsel someone at an evangelistic crusade.

And the one-to-one approach does seem to be what is bringing people to church. In a survey of twenty-two congregations in three major cities, newcomers were asked, "What brought you to this church?" Roy Oswald reports the following responses:

> 2 percent—an advertisement
> 6 percent—an invitation by the pastor
> 6 percent—an organized evangelistic outreach program
> 86 percent—an invitation by a friend or family member[9]

In a seminar format, Herb Miller says that people are more responsive to invitations from church members than they were ten years ago. Today 63 percent of Americans feel positive about receiving an invitation to a church; that's compared to only 52 percent in the early 1980s.

These statistics reveal that relational evangelism has replaced mass evangelism as the primary method of evangelism. Notice that in 86 percent of the cases, the invitation came from a "friend" and not just a "someone." Steve Sjogren claims, "It seems people don't necessarily remember what they are told of God's love, but they never forget what they have experienced of God's love."[10] Door-to-door evangelism is more about "telling," while relational evangelism is more about "experiencing."

It may take several experiences with God before a person is ready to make a commitment to God. Most often, potential converts need at least five significant encounters with the gospel before accepting Jesus as Savior.[11] For people to "buy" anything, at one time they had to be exposed to a product at least seven times: seven times for a sale. "Today," I was recently informed by a public relations person, "people need at least twelve exposures." Gone are the days when a single evangelist can grow a church numerically. One Christian in a single community simply cannot provide enough encounters for a multitude of people to experience Jesus Christ several different times. Today it requires the efforts of many Christians working together in a relational evangelism approach to help a church grow numerically. Most people would rather hear about Jesus from a friend than from a stranger or a professional.

Theoretical Support

Why are people more likely to respond to a personal invitation than they would to an invitation given en masse? The wording of this question nearly gives us our answer. By nature we humans seem to want to be noticed, included, and cared for. Many have great reservations about this kind of true caring taking place inside a church. Why? Partly because the church is viewed as an institution. People in society have become skeptical about the motives and promises of institutions. Schools promised an education. The government promised peace. Colleges promised a job. Many baby boomers (people born from 1946 to 1964) do not believe that institutions have lived up to their promises.

"A substantial number of persons are not seeking out churches on their own initiative. By and large, persons live life as though the church does not substantially matter."[12] A large portion of baby boomers have grown up with a negative experience of church. These negative experiences range from memories of parents dropping children off at church and never attending themselves to memories of painful church fights being rehashed among their parents and parents' friends. What happens when these negative experiences are carried into the next generation? The next generation that comes along does not experience any negative feelings toward the church. Nor do they experience any positive feelings! The next generation of parents that comes along chooses not to go to church. This scenario is obviously not accurate in all circumstances. But it is accurate often enough that there are probably a lot more people in your neighborhood than you realize who know nothing about church. Nothing about Jesus Christ. Many cannot be approached via any other evangelistic strategy than relational evangelism.

Examples of churches failing to attract people in their community can be found in every geographical arena. Even Florida! Many pastors think this locale to be safe from the nationwide decline in church membership. Not so, points out Schaller:

> Today the number of retirees and winter visitors on Florida's west coast is several times what it was in 1957, but the February attendance at many of these churches is less than one-half what it was three or four decades earlier.[13]

These churches are attracting a few more retirees, but they do not appear to be attracting people from a broad base of their community. Florida churches are not that different from other states in their failure to attract people from all fragments of their neighborhoods. In 1987 mainline denominations included 45 percent of American Protestants born during the 1920s, but only 28 percent of those born during the 1960s.[14]

If the church of tomorrow begins to act more like a first-century church than a twentieth-century church (as discussed in chapter 2), it must turn its focus of evangelism away from inside the church walls and out into the community. The first-century church practiced evangelism by holding conversations with people where they lived rather than by evangelistic worship services.[15]

Naisbitt points out that the recent increase in technology exacerbates the need for reaching out to people where they live and showing them that the church cares. Naisbitt coined the term "high tech/high touch" to account for this need:

The more technology we introduce into society, the more people will aggregate, will want to be with other people: at movies, rock concerts, shopping. Shopping malls, for example, are now the third most frequented space in our lives, following home and workplace.[16]

Notice that the church is not in the top three of the most frequented places in America! Naisbitt later adds, "You do not go to a movie just to see a movie. You go to a movie to cry or laugh with 200 other people."[17] I think it is fascinating that the invention of the home video cassette player/recorder (VCR) has not replaced the activity of attending movies. People will pay two or three times the price of a rental to watch a movie in a theater. People still want to feel connected.

People want to know you care. People want to receive invitations to church from people they know. People want to be introduced to God, and be invited to hear more about God from people who are already their friends.

People in the church need to appear to others as being caring and compassionate. The entire church should also give that signal.

Some have suggested that one characteristic of growing churches is that they transcend their denominations. (Every denomination will present certain barriers to certain people.) Posterski demonstrates this concept in an illustration about Mother Teresa. He states that on numerous occasions, he has asked audiences to make word-association responses to the images that they hold of Mother Teresa. He reports:

On no occasion has anyone said "Roman Catholic" or even "a nun." Mother Teresa has transcended her organizational identity. The perceptions around Mother Teresa are partly explained by the trends of our time. We are in a culture that believes more in people than in organizations.[18]

It's okay for people in your community to know that you are a Baptist church, or a Methodist church, or a Presbyterian church. But first they should know and think of your church as a caring church.

Anecdotal Support

The statistics and theories being published today present a world hungering for relationships rather than for institutions. People in the trenches are singing the same song. A recent issue of *Christianity Today* presents a story of evangelism over the computer waves.

Lori Skillman, a sophomore at Cedarville College in Ohio, was conversing on the Internet, a communication link for computers. She had apparently communicated back and forth several times with someone who lived several states away from her. She and her acquaintance conversed via words that traveled across her computer screen, across the phone lines, and finally across her recipient's computer screen. One particular day, back came this reply:

> I've been bashing your God, but you haven't run away; you haven't condemned me. Nobody has ever listened to me like this before. I want that kind of peace in my life, that kind of calm.

Skillman's computer reply palpitated back to her new companion, traversing the 2,500 miles in seconds, "That's God in me." She proceeded to tell her friend, whom she had never met in person, about the good news of Jesus Christ. Her friend began a relationship with the Lord that day. Later he admitted to her, "That was the first time I've cried for any reason."[19]

This example may be the ultimate demonstration of a high tech/high touch world. People today are starving for a relationship with someone real. People have a void in their lives that cannot be filled by technology. Skillman ministered to her friend by being compassionate, honest, and caring, even through the use of her computer.

I can still recall the moment when my Armenian college roommate answered my question, "What have you got planned for spring break?" with, "I'm going to go out and buy a Bible and see what it's all about." He said he had been thinking about this for a long time as a result of some conversations we had had about the possibility of my entering seminary. I had not "witnessed" to him in the sense of explaining the good news of Jesus Christ. But I had talked about good news from God that I was personally experiencing. My roommate told me that he had never previously opened a Bible, but that he had been secretly reading mine when I was away at class. His relationship with God started as a result of hearing about a friend's relationship with God. Relational evangelism is just that. It is sharing our own relationship with God with another who already calls us friend. Relational evangelism involves making one of our friends Christ's friend.

People long for someone to converse with them at their level. Without judgment. Without ulterior motives. Without a canned speech. A friend of mine and I recently discussed evangelism in today's world. He had been trained to evangelize strangers using specific methods—through a program titled Evangelism Explosion. He told me he had led numerous people to Christ over the years, but that the only people "who really stuck with it" were those with whom he already had previous contact. "Not one person," he said, "has ever gone on to become a church member whom I originally approached using Evangelism Explosion techniques."

The sincerity may be there in seeking to care for the present and future well-being of people we know and people we do not know, but it appears that people we already know are better able to feel the sincerity come across. I was once told during a Billy Graham School of Evangelism session I was attending that an estimated one-half of the people who walk down the aisle at Billy Graham Crusades give false name and address information when asked to fill out their information cards. This piece of evidence suggests to me that even people who have just made a decision to commit their lives to Jesus Christ, and who may have been invited to the crusade by a friend, are uneasy about being contacted later on by a stranger. Mass evangelism may have enabled a lot of people to learn about and make a commitment to God. But relational evangelism provides a ready-made opportunity for the new convert to grow in Christ with a friend. That difference is significant.

Relational evangelism means getting involved in the lives of other people. Not by meddling in their affairs but by caring about them and their involvements.

At times the church and society are worlds apart. I have served my current church for eight years. But only in the last year have I been faced with opportunities to visit members in jail, speak at an Alcoholics Anonymous meeting, appear in the courtroom as a character witness for a member, and baptize two people living together who had come to me for premarital counseling for a wedding this fall.

Why all of this in the last year and not before? I don't know. It could be a sign that we are beginning to bridge some distance from what may have existed between our church and this community. It could be that it took eight years for people to understand fully that I would accept them no matter what. It could be that the longer I am in this community, the greater the expansion of relational evangelism opportunities.

Because society and the church are diverging, as detailed in chapter two, the people who choose to become linked to the church and distance themselves from society will have a strong need for acceptance within the church. That acceptance is best communicated through relationships that matter with the people around us.

Theological Support

I believe many Americans are unknowingly seeking out my God as someone with whom they can talk and build a relationship. They have no idea that a Spirit called Christ is trying to communicate with them just as forcefully as they are trying to communicate with Christ. God has the ability to appeal to someone who has had no previous encounter with Christianity and who has never had anyone talk to them about God. I think of Paul's words to the people on Mars Hill: "What you worship in ignorance, we proclaim to you" (Acts 17:23).

We, as Christians, have a tremendous opportunity to proclaim God to people outside our churches who have already been worshipping our God, but who, out of a sense of ignorance or lack of knowledge, do not know God. There are a great number of people in America whose parents never took them to church. And many have had a negative experience with a church as their only introduction to the people of God; they have never been properly introduced to our God.

In Ephesians 2:19, we read, "So then you are no longer strangers and aliens, but you are citizens with the saints and also members of the household of God." This today is the good news that our society longs to hear.

Jesus befriended people. Mass evangelism and relational evangelism are both biblical. But mass evangelism without some form of relational follow-up may not be. I believe that the church has been presented with an opportunity to do evangelism the way it was done in the first century, by demonstrating God's love to our friends.

We are created in the image of God. When we choose to become children of God, we are given an additional role of being stewards of God's image. When Joseph interpreted Pharaoh's dream, he was given the job of Pharaoh's chief steward. Later his brothers suggested that Joseph had become just like Pharaoh. We are not and will never be just like God. But could we be so identified with God, by carrying God's image into the world, that the world might choose to call us Christians, with new respect for the Word, seeing the image of Christ in our love for them?

Paul told the Corinthian church that they were to be God's letter in the world (2 Cor. 3:2). You may be as close to God as your friend will ever get, unless you reveal God's image to your friend. What kind of managers have we been as stewards of God's image? What kind of managers of God's image will the churches be, as we head toward a new kind of church in the next millennium?

Where We Begin

Discussing the Trend

1. What do you think of when you hear the word evangelism? What do you think of when you hear the word friendship?
2. How were you first introduced to Jesus Christ? Ask several people in a variety of age ranges the same question. Do any patterns emerge?
3. When was the last time your church held an evangelistic crusade? What were the results?
4. When was the last time your church had a visitation night? What were the results?
5. What other evangelistic activities has your church attempted? Did these activities focus upon the masses or upon individual people?
6. Where do the majority of your new members come from?

Applying the Trend

1. Conduct an analysis of the ages of your members. Is there any age
    group that you are failing to reach?
2. Visit other churches to discover how they are appealing to their
    community. Obtain a list of churches to visit from your denomina-
    tion.
3. Begin to develop a strategy of how to apply the four levels of
    relational evangelism detailed in this chapter. Hold a retreat to
    develop such a strategy.

CHAPTER FOUR

From Tribal Education to Immigrant Education

At one time the primary focus of Christian education was teaching the basics of our faith to the children and youth within the church. If that is all a church does today, it will receive a poor grade for its educational ministries.

In the past churches educated their members as if they were educating members of a tribe. In terms of religious culture, those teaching were very similar to those learning. Today churches need to view their educational ministries as the education of immigrants who have chosen to move onto their soil with little, if any, previous knowledge of the land and its people. Churches are shifting from tribal education to immigrant education.

Although this shift has affected the entire spectrum of Christian education, its impact has been felt most deeply in two dominant areas: discipling new members and providing life-long learning experiences for people at different stages in their faith development.

Where We've Been

In previous years Christian education was similar to American public education in its early years. Educating people in a church was like educating children in a one-room schoolhouse. Everybody knew everybody else. Most new members to the one-room schoolhouse were first graders. They were new because they had not been old enough to go to school the previous year. A new member coming onto the scene in some other manner was big news. If the new member was from a different culture, it was really big news.

In the one-room schoolhouse, new members were very similar to old members. They possessed many of the same heroes and champions as the group they joined. They had similar values. The communities were homogeneous and so were their educational environments. Certain items did not have to be taught. It was safe to make assumptions. Before new schoolchildren ever entered the door, they knew that respecting elders would be a common thread in the fabric of the rules. They also knew that discipline would be the primary means of enforcing rules. They knew when the holidays would come. They knew that school would be cut short to help with the harvest. Before coming to school, they were probably already acquainted with the teacher, not just by name. Teachers could daily delve into the real stuff of reading, writing, and arithmetic because little else was required prior to teaching those subjects.

In many ways Christian education was simpler when it could be compared to education in a one-room schoolhouse. It was simpler because it involved more training than educating. Much of the base of religious education had already been provided by parents. In those years people in a particular church learned more about their church and denomination from their ancestors than from the church leadership. That no longer holds. Christian education was simpler then because, before joining the church, new members often already knew several of the church members and church principles. Today new members must be not only educated, but also assimilated. Christian education was easier when it consisted primarily of educating children and youth, rather than parents and grandparents. Many adults do not want to confess a need to be educated in Christianity 101. It feels like starting all over in something. It is.

Although there are still 376 one-room schoolhouses in Nebraska and a host in other states as well, most are not used anymore.[1] Today's educational methods simply do not fare well in a one-room schoolhouse. Yet the structures still dot the landscape as reminders of what once was. Many church buildings are also dotted with reminders of the past: sanctuaries with a rail down the middle for separating men and women, enough Sunday school class rooms for a boys' and girls' class in each grade, a room used exclusively for Sunday school "opening exercises," a piano in every classroom. Some educational programs will have to work around the old structures, trying not to allow old structures to hinder new strategies for education.

Where We're Headed

Christian education is in the midst of a transition. I remember hearing
Garrison Keillor on public radio describing children's ability to elicit fear
in adults. "Children love to scream," he suggested, "for the sheer pleas-
ure of seeing immense people move fast." He told a story—one day
when he and his sister thought their mom must be upstairs. "M-O-O-O-
O-O-O-M!" they screamed. Down the stairs she bounded. To hear the
grown Keillor tell it, he was more intent on seeing how fast his mother
could travel down the stairs than on what he was going to say when he
met her terrified face. "Pretty good wheels for a big woman," Keillor
told his audience.

One can picture the look of dismay on the parent's face—discovering that this blood-curdling scream had been motivated by curiosity
rather than pain. Pain probably quickly became a part of the picture.

Today's Christian educators experience similar shock. One of our
newest church members has yelled up the staircase of nostalgia request-
ing a routine course in Christian education. Down the long stairway the
Christian educator plunges, only to discover that the old set of assumptions about how to tackle this problem will no longer work.

One can no longer assume that the person seeking Christian education will already know the heroes of the instructor's particular faith. The
learner might not even know where to find the Book of Hebrews in the
Bible, let alone the book of Habakkuk! The learner might know nothing
of the denomination's first foreign missionaries. Nothing about the or-
dinances or the offerings. Not even the words to the favorite hymns of
the church. Nor the tune. Times have changed.

We are no longer educating tribal members who have arrived for
their token rite of passage. Church members must now be educated as if
they were immigrants, receiving a comprehensive curriculum from the
church. Many pieces of information once assumed to be a part of every
new member's vocabulary are no longer already present in the minds of
the learners; they must be taught.

And it is often difficult to teach what one takes for granted. Isn't that
why methods courses are so important for elementary school teachers
even though the teachers already know how to read and write? What
about methods courses for immigrant education? We turn to that subject
next.

Tribal education assumes that the people to be trained come into the process with a certain amount of knowledge. Immigrant education assumes nothing. Churches today are discovering that they can no longer assume that their new members will know the hymns of their worship, the ideals of their church, the distinctives of their heritage, the roots of their mission, or the founders of their denomination.

Two well-known leaders have practiced immigrant education for years in radically differing ways. Billy Graham has never assumed that his hearers already knew the content of the gospel prior to coming to one of his meetings. William Sloan Coffin has never assumed that his hearers already knew how to live out the gospel and perform social ministry prior to coming to his church. More and more people are coming to churches with less and less knowledge of the church. So it doesn't matter whether a church is trying to promote discipleship, social ministry, or any other aspect; immigrant education is the means to get there.

What are the methods of immigrant education? Let's look at mentoring, assimilation, and life-long learning.

Mentoring

Warren Bennis writes, "I know of no leader in any era who hasn't had at least one mentor: a teacher who found things in him he didn't know were there."[2] Mentoring provides the person being mentored with an opportunity to dispel a basic set of beliefs, a collection of tools that can be used in a variety of settings, and a way of life, all of which are needed by many people who join churches today. Mentoring differs from teaching by involving the student and teacher in an honest and respectful relationship. Many teachers are wonderful mentors, but not all. To put it in Venn diagram language straight out of logic 101: All mentors are teachers, but not all teachers are mentors.

In a good mentoring relationship, two people are able to discuss any topic. Nothing is "off limits." That kind of relationship is greatly needed today. Many new members need a "safe place" where they can ask questions about developing their faith. Tough questions. Embarrassing questions. Silly questions. Questions that would never be posed without a safe space in which to ask them.

The ideal process would be to assign every new church member to a mentor and then sit back and watch the bonding take place. The problem with this prescription is that it does not work. For obvious reasons. Bonding occurs naturally between a newborn and a parent, but it does not always occur naturally between two adults. Think back to the mentors you have had in your life. How many were assigned to you through some institutional process? A few times an institution will get lucky doing this, but luck, by definition, will not produce a 100 percent yield.

For the most part the mentors in my life were not assigned. The relationships were sought out and nurtured by both sides. In my experience the best mentoring relationships have been based on a kind of providence, or even kismet, a kindred spirit between the mentor and the mentee. This kind of bond is impossible to conjure up through an assignment process akin to a computer dating service.

Let me clarify my argument at this point. First of all, I believe that every new member in the church needs mentoring, whether the person is a new Christian, new to this denomination, or simply new to the community. Assigning a new member to a person who is asked to shepherd, mentor, or guide the new member is a good idea. But it is unrealistic to expect that every assignment will result in a good mentoring relationship. So in addition to any formal mentoring process that the church chooses to establish, the church should promote mentoring relationships and foster opportunities for new members to get acquainted with older members.

In board meetings talk about the importance of mentoring relationships. Teach about it. Preach about it. Encourage it. Expect mentoring relationships to form. Encourage every member of your church regularly to greet visitors and new members. Encourage existing small groups to welcome new members. Regularly form new small groups made up of new members. Kismet cannot be manipulated, but increasing the number of opportunities for new members to meet old members and for new members to meet each other will increase the opportunities for mentoring relationships to form.

Assimilation

Assimilation is the process of involving a new member more deeply in the life of the local church. The first step in the assimilation process is to provide a forum for new members to learn the basics about your church and denomination. Many churches have held new members' classes for years. But in providing new member assimilation immigrant-style, the critical question is this: How can we provide an introduction to our church and denomination that assumes nothing? What previous knowledge does your new members' class assume? Is there time set aside within the new members' class to discuss the elements of your worship service; what a Bible is, where it came from, and where to find things in it; the roles of a trustee, elder, deacon, presbytery, or whatever other offices are held in your church? Many new members are afraid to admit to anyone that they do not know the doxology, the Lord's Prayer, where to find Luke, or other basics. Without a class that lays out these basics, many would never learn the basics because they would never feel comfortable enough to seek out answers.

The second step in assimilation is to encourage and provide opportunities for new members to join small groups. Small groups include the choir, the softball team, Bible study groups, mothers' groups, youth groups, seniors' groups, Sunday school classes, and any other group in your church that meets on a regular basis. Only through analysis can your church discover which of these groups are open to new members. All of them will say that they welcome new people. But not all of them regularly add new members.

Your church does not have to be organized around small groups to encourage small groups. The cell group movement is an excellent way to assimilate new members into your church. The philosophy behind this movement is to provide a similar small group experience for every member of your congregation. New cells are formed regularly as new members join. But this is not the only way to form small groups and clearly not the only way to assimilate new members.

Every person in your church has a need to feel a part of some group, but it need not be a cell group. Boards, committees, task force groups, ad hoc groups, ministry groups, educational groups, and fellowship groups all fulfill this purpose. If you do not pursue the route of cell groups, provide many other, varied opportunities for new members to feel connected. Once a part of a group, the new member will no doubt continue to explore the deeper meanings of faith.

One might ask, "Small groups are certainly not new. We have had Sunday school classes for a century. How are small groups a part of

some new trend called immigrant education?" I answer by saying that
the people joining the small groups are changing. It requires a great deal
of courage to join a group of people who know more than you, come
from a different culture than you, or are from a different generation. If
your existing small groups have been regularly adding new members,
you have found ways to bridge these gaps that have formed over the
years. If they are not regularly adding new participants, your church
must find another way to assimilate new members into a small group
setting.

New small groups may be formed around issues that would interest
the joining members. New Sunday school classes may be started. New
Bible study discussion groups may be formed. New ministries or task
forces may be started. Every new member needs to feel that there are
opportunities to get involved with a small group of people. Roberta
Hestenes provides an excellent resource for forming small groups in the
church. Her book *Using the Bible in Groups* recommends topics, for-
mats, time schedules, and contracts among participants and gives many
other helpful pieces of advice.[3]

Life-Long Learning

Immigrant education also involves providing educational opportunities
for church members to learn at every stage of their faith development. Is
your church meeting the needs of brand new Christians? Is it finding
ways to challenge mature Christians? How similar are your church
members' theologies? If the answer is "very similar," you might reflect
on the opportunities provided to members to develop their faith. Sometimes many church members' theologies are similar because they all
have felt compelled to copy the theologies of the church leaders. People
are unique in many ways, including the ways they develop their faith.
Immigrant education recognizes this uniqueness.

Varied opportunities for spiritual growth lead to varied paths of faith
development. Do you offer topical Bible studies? Do you provide spiritual counseling? Spirituality retreats? Does your church leadership
model meditational times with God?

Often a crisis will prompt a person to advance from one stage of faith
development to another. I recently talked to a person who had dropped

out of church life immediately after experiencing a broken relationship. His theology had not allowed him to make sense of the crisis. "I had prayed for a mate. God had given her to me and then took her away." Because of his old theology, he chose to ignore God rather than expand his view of God. His faith had been heavy on the Calvinist or predestination side of the predestination-free will continuum. When I suggested that God may have been just as disappointed as he over the broken relationship, it seemed to unleash a whole new view of God. He went away eager to explore and redevelop his theology, ready to progress from one stage of faith to another.

One need not have a highly intellectual vocabulary regarding stages of faith development to assist another along faith's journey. Good listening skills and an open mind toward God are more important than any concrete knowledge. Knowledge, however, is never a hindrance in this area. Various theories of faith and life development will be introduced, but not detailed, in the theoretical support section of this chapter. For further study in this area, please consult the bibliography.

Learning from the Immigrants

One reason our country has such a great resource of abilities and skills available in its citizens is directly related to its cultural diversity. From my group dynamics training I recall that the greater the diversity within a group, the longer the group will take to bond and begin functioning as a team—but then that diverse team has the benefit of a larger resource-skills base. The same is true on a national scale and in local churches. As the diversity within a church's membership increases, education will be more difficult, but ministry opportunities also will be greater if the educational leaders take time to get to know the ones being educated. Many teachers in Christian education feel they learn as much from their students as they give to their students.

Today's churches need to take more time in educating—and listening to—the people joining their ranks. "The church learns to sing with the songs of the past, but each generation must sing its own mission."[4] Churches must give their new members enough time and safe space to develop their own songs of faith in this foreign land of ours.

Statistical Support

Lydia Saad reports that 23 percent of Americans have changed religions or denominations.[5] Change is higher among Protestants than Catholics. Studies also show that those who convert to a new denomination are usually more religious than those who remain in the same denomination.[6] These statistics reinforce not only the difficulty of the task of Christian education, but also its rewards. People who join a church today may know less than in previous generations, but they are actually more eager to learn.

Theoretical Support

Immigrant education is education in the purest sense of the word. Tribal education was closer to training. Bennis theorizes about the differences between education and training.[7] Note some of these differences below:

Education	Training
inductive	deductive
dynamic	static
understanding	memorizing
broad	narrow
experiential	rote
active	passive
process	content
discovery	dogma
active	reactive
long-term	short-term
risk	rules
synthesis	thesis
open	closed
imagination	common sense

Education operates from an entirely different perspective than training. So does immigrant and tribal education. The differences are crucial. Immigrant education will facilitate individual development throughout one's entire life. Tribal education is simply adding one more program to the church composite.

A person progressing through educational experiences within the church will no doubt advance through various stages of development. One may view the "stages of life" through multifaceted lenses, but even to mention the concept of "stages" funnels us into the world of cognitive development, a world guided by at least three assumptions. Jean Piaget is most often credited with setting the tone for later cognitive development theories.[8] He originally set forth these assumptions:

1. *Structural organization.* People actively interpret the outside world. People reflect upon their experiences. They filter information. They develop patterns or schemes to make sense of their world.
2. *Developmental sequence.* People develop according to stages. People make progress along a continuum. Each stage represents a different way of thinking.
3. *Interactionism.* People make progress as a direct result of the interaction with their environments. Individual people are confronted by environmental stimuli that they can no longer explain using an old model. This provides dissonance or disequilibrium, forcing the individual to progress to a new stage.

Many people have theorized about life development using these three assumptions. William Perry talks of intellectual and ethical development using the stages of dualism, multiplicity, relativism, and commitment in relativism.[9] Lawrence Kohlberg discusses stages of moral reasoning.[10] James Fowler talks of stages of faith. DiGiacomo and Walsh present ten stages of Christian discovery.[11] No matter how you label the stages, Piaget provides the framework for the labels. The truth is that people do develop through stages of life. For a Christian education program to be successful today, it must recognize that people progress through various stages of faith development during their lives. One role of immigrant education is to provide both the stimuli of dissonance and the safe space for exploring new stages.

Anecdotal Support

I still remember the discipleship class I attended at the age of eight.
Everyone in the class was already my friend. All of our parents were
active members of the same church. We knew the pastor by name, as
well as the associate pastor, and the deacon who addressed our class one
Sunday to discuss opportunities for service within the church. At the age
of eight, I already knew how to sing the doxology. I knew when to sit
and when to rise during a worship service. I knew that the cup and those
funny little wafers would be handed out the first Sunday of every month.

The new members' class I recently taught in the church I pastor was
radically different from the first discipleship class I attended. A Methodist, a Southern Baptist, a person who had previously attended the Church
of God, and a couple who had never attended church in their forty-two
years of marriage were among the participants. I could make no assumptions regarding previous knowledge of worship, doctrine, denominational
distinctives, or theology.

Teaching the basics of the Christian faith to a diverse group of people is an arduous task. Encouraging that same diverse group to grow into
mature knowledgeable Christian critical thinkers is even more difficult.
Many Christian curricula written today are not geared to an intellectually
and spiritually diverse group.

Partly due to my disappointment in available materials and partly
due to my adventuresome spirit, I designed a curriculum for the same
diverse group who had completed the new members' class described
above. To my surprise, nearly everyone invited agreed to participate.
I designed the lessons around fourteen topics I believed every Christian
should eventually come to grips with. I began by brainstorming with a
different Bible study group about the fourteen most important issues for
a Christian to understand. Our list included obedience to God, communion, stewardship, evangelism, salvation, unity, the church, prayer, faith,
baptism, ministry, the Holy Spirit, scripture, and daily living.

Next, I asked the same Bible study group, "What stories in the Bible
best teach about these issues?" In asking this question my expectations
were quite grand and quite unrealistic. I expected the stories chosen to
teach the concepts, and I had hoped the class members would later be
able to remember the concepts by recalling the stories. In the movie
Silent Fall, actor Richard Dreyfuss speaks of a uniform pathway that

must be followed to unlock an autistic child's memory to a particular event. I had hoped that, in the future, members of the class could unlock a wealth of understanding about a particular concept simply by recalling one Bible story.

We had some scintillating discussions. And the class was a success. Its success, however, was due to all of the positive side-effects that resulted from the class, not because my two original hopes were met. The class spawned new relationships. The class created a hungering to learn more about the Christian faith. The Bible was presented as a book that is alive with current application. But the stories suggested by the Bible study group members often gave rise to an entirely different point than the one I had hoped the discipleship group would discuss each meeting. Stories, by themselves, were not enough to enlighten one about a particular concept or to serve as a pathway for remembering that concept in the future.

Morton Kelsey presents a much more in-depth model for Christian growth. Kelsey's model has been field tested and proven to be helpful.[12] Kelsey began with the premise that educating Christians is as important as anything else a local church can do, including preaching and financing new buildings. Classes were limited to fifteen. Every member paid a small fee to attend. Anyone who was consistently late or absent without good reason was dropped from the class. The seminar method became the primary means of instruction because it allowed students to bring a familiar concept, as well as a list of questions and doubts, into group interaction. According to Kelsey, the seminar method also creates teachers, "Those who become most deeply involved in the classes are soon able to conduct a class themselves."[13] I was intrigued to hear that each initial group studied material now contained in Kelsey's book *Encounter with God*. This same book served as a catalyst for an entire reformation of my own personal views about spirituality, views that I will disclose in chapter 6. Subsequent courses focused on the Old and New Testaments, theology, and so forth.

Conducting immigrant education is no easy task. It cannot be accomplished via business as usual. Catholics now rate the activity of bingo above Christian education.[14] I wonder if Protestants would rate refreshments above Sunday school? In many areas real education has become as rare within Christian education programs as the practice of keeping one's gloves in the glove compartment. Tomorrow's churches have two choices. They can keep on fooling themselves into thinking that they are meeting the educational needs of their members with homogeneous methods that are successful only with homogeneous members, or they can begin to acknowledge the diverse needs of their heterogeneous members and build an immigrant education program from the ground up.

Theological Support

Many Christians today are not ready for solid food. The problem lies not so much in the availability of the food, but in the ability of the church to serve it properly. A good main course should be offered only after a good appetizer. Proper utensils should also be provided along with enough liquid to "wash it down."

Jesus knew all about mentoring, assimilation, and life-long learning. Jesus trained a group of twelve and then sent them out. He trained a group of seventy and then sent them out. Jesus always called, mentored, and then sent, in that precise order.

Jesus' disciples called him Rabbi. Jesus was an educator and took that role very seriously. Jesus presented the gospel to all types of people without ever sugar-coating it. Many churches today would drool over the prospect of having a rich young ruler join their church. "Make sure you visit that new young politician in the neighborhood," a pastor's parishioners would encourage, with no thought regarding the lawyer's commitment to Christ. Jesus, on the other hand, sent away a rich young ruler until such a time when the ruler could commit to Jesus fully, with nothing else standing in the way. Jesus broke down the barriers to presenting the gospel but never splintered the gospel itself. Tomorrow's churches must discover productive means of teaching the diverse set of people who will come to them seeking the Lord. Some of these means may be radically different from the old, but each new method must present the same Jesus whom the pillars of the church have come to know well. How can this next generation of learners know Jesus like the last generation? That is the task before us. I believe it is the task of immigrant education.

Where We Begin

Discussing the Trend

1. Who have been your mentors in life? Were any of them assigned to you through some institutional process? How else have mentoring relationships formed in your life?
2. What spiritual needs did you have at the ages of eight? Twelve? Eighteen? Twenty-nine? Forty-nine? Sixty-five? Seventy-five? Ninety?
3. Does your church provide more training or education to its new members? To its existing members?
4. Approximately what percentage of your church members have been assimilated into a small group?

Applying the Trend

1. Does your church have a new members' class? Spend some time evaluating the curriculum for this class. Has the curriculum changed in the last decade or two? If not, should it be altered? In what ways? What previous knowledge does the curriculum assume that the participants will have?
2. Compile a list of the newest members of your church. What do they have in common? What is their church background? What is the profile of the people who are joining your church?
3. List all of the small groups in your church. Which ones regularly add new members? Poll each of your small groups to uncover this information. What do your results reveal?
4. Brainstorm to compile a list of at least five possible small groups that could be started within your church. Make plans to commence two of the five during the coming year.
5. Write the following stages of life on a sheet of newsprint in columns: childhood, adolescence, young adulthood, marriage, singleness, divorce, parenting, career expansion, empty nest, retirement, caregiving, facing death. Under each column, list the activities or ministries that your church is currently providing to assist people in this stage of life. Draw a horizontal line underneath your list. Now

brainstorm about other activities that could be introduced into the life-long educational ministries of your church.

6. Invite someone to make a presentation to your church regarding the stages of life development.
7. If you are a pastor, have you ever considered preaching a sermon series on mentoring?
8. If you are a layperson, where in your church might you offer to lead a workshop on mentoring?

CHAPTER FIVE

From Surrogate Missions to Hands-On Missions

The focus of ministry is changing. The primary reason for this is the change in relationship between the church and society. When society was fully supportive of the church, the church saw little need to minister to the society. Now that society and church are so different, many churches sense a new compelling urge to do more ministry in their own neighborhoods. This trend toward localized ministry is also driven by a powerful urge to get involved in ministry with one's whole self rather than with just one's purse.

Where We've Been

What is a missionary? Not long ago a mainline Protestant church member would respond: someone who takes a boat to a far-away country, learns a language that no one else in the world speaks, eats strange food, and then works for years to try to get at least one person to understand and accept Jesus. Missions was viewed as something launched beyond the sights of a local church, bypassing the immediate neighborhood, and hitting its target in some foreign land.

Foreign mission boards were formed to send out missionaries on behalf of local churches. For many years missions was performed out of a fiduciary relationship between foreign mission boards and local churches. Local churches certainly did not need to send missionaries into their own neighborhoods; there all they had to do was open the church doors and let the people in. So local churches could fulfill the Great Commission without getting directly involved. This model was "sold" by a group that needed the money and "bought" by a group that needed its conscience appeased. It was a fair trade but never an adequate theological model for missions. Even when local churches were sending out foreign missionaries by the multitudes, they still should have maintained a mission interest in their own neighborhoods. But sending money is sometimes easier than sending anything else.

All along the way, a small minority of pastors and theologians continued to advocate for both hands-on and localized ministries. One of Martin Luther's ninety-five theses was "Christians are to be taught that to give to the poor or to lend to the needy is a better work than the purchase of pardons."[1] Luther, and others who have followed in his footsteps, have promoted the performance of ministry rather than the purchase of ministry. Today's trend toward hands-on ministry is a good trend, but of the seven trends in this book, it will be the slowest to be fully implemented. The dominant "I don't want to get involved" attitude of the seventies and eighties will not disappear all at once.

During the surrogate missions era, churches cocooned in their sanctuaries for several reasons. First, society was so much like the local church that it didn't need missionaries. Once the American West was settled and civilized, there was a strong societal belief that people overseas needed Jesus much more than did the people in America.

Second, it was viewed as the spiritual thing to do:

When being a Christian became synonymous with being a citizen, many in the church became convinced that to really be Christian, to really fulfill one's calling in Christ, one had to withdraw from the world at large and seek a controlled environment.[2]

Third, the clear distinction between clergy and laity suggested that any hands-on ministry performed was to be done by the pastor, the professional in the arena of ministry. More about this subject in chapter 7.

Fourth, somewhere along the line, the various components of personal Christian growth were compartmentalized and presented as options rather than necessities. The church forgot that a part of a person's growth as a Christian would never materialize until that person got involved in a hands-on ministry, developed a responsibility for stewardship and giving, and practiced worship as an individual and not just corporately with others. Along with deepening one's spirituality, tithing, and Bible study, hands-on ministry became an option rather than a requirement for being a Christian. Simply to show up in a church on a semiregular basis seemed to fulfill the minimum weekly requirements of being a Christian; anything else was dessert, including hands-on ministry.

Where We're Headed

The old trend is for churches to delegate their mission tasks to their denomination. The new trend is for churches to get physically, emotionally, and spiritually involved in their mission responsibility, for churches to play a more dynamic role in the mission enterprise. The new trend is toward hands-on ministry. There are two primary reasons for this trend. The first relates to newly developed opportunities for ministry. The second relates to a motivation to get involved in and support these new opportunities.

A Matter of Opportunity

Kennon Callahan declares, "The day of the churched culture is over; the day of the mission field has come."[3] The Christendom Paradigm, discussed in chapter two, was characterized by a friendly and supportive environment beyond the immediate walls of church buildings. The Christendom Paradigm is giving way toward a new paradigm in which the immediate environment of the local church is once again ambivalent toward the church. Today all churches, like the first-century churches, are beginning to face a hostile environment at their doorstep. The hostile environment means that America is now a mission field.

The neighborhoods of America have become more culturally and ethnically diverse. Many people who have come to America from other lands have never heard of Jesus Christ. Opportunities to evangelize, disciple, and minister to people of diverse backgrounds abound in America. Vietnamese boat people, Haitian refugees, the sanctuary movement, and the Golden Venture have all contributed to the opportunities to evangelize the world in America. "In 1970, 4.7% of America was foreign born. Today, at least 8% is."[4] Now that the mission field has come to America, opportunities are even greater than in the past for churches that wish to evangelize the world. It is extremely difficult to take the gospel to people who are fully supported by their own cultural and religious background. As people come to America, however, they leave their religious support network. Once free from peer and familial pressure to resist, immigrants are potentially more open to accepting a new religion.

There are also more opportunities to witness to Americans born in this country. More and more people who have been born in America have never heard of Jesus Christ! Recall from chapter three that negative experiences have kept many of today's baby boomers out of the church. Churches today are faced with the task of discovering new ways of appealing to a new generation.

A Matter of Motivation

The trend toward hands-on ministry could never have become a trend with opportunity alone. It had to be driven by something. People pass up opportunities to get involved in wonderful activities every day of their lives. Even good Christian people. The trend toward hands-on ministry was instigated by opportunity. It was fueled, however, by the motivating factors of trust and distance. The business of financially supporting foreign and national missionaries has been hindered by scandals on the part of a few mission agencies. Fiscal scandals linked to Jim Bakker and even United Way opened the door of skepticism toward all collecting agents of mission dollars. Today many senders of mission dollars mistrust the receivers of those dollars.

Trust is not the greatest factor, however, driving the trend toward hands-on ministry. Distance is. The primary confidence factor relates more to distance than to competency in personnel. The distance between the person giving the money to foreign missions and the foreign missionary directly affected the acquiescence of the missionary supporter sitting in the pew. Many local churches in mainline denominations have been distanced from their foreign and national missionaries. In some communities, it is becoming easier to support the captain of the Salvation Army with whom you drink a cup of coffee at the coffee shop every morning than it is to support someone in your own denomination whom you have never met. Once mistrust opened the door of skepticism, the fear of distance drove the train of doubt fully across the threshold.

The decline in denominational loyalty also did not help. Church members today may not care about the denominational affiliation of the local person erecting a haven for abused victims, putting up a home for the homeless, or building a rain shelter for the neighborhood children as they wait for the school bus. When the giver can see the structure escalating board by board and brick by brick, and can even talk to the people placing the boards and bricks, the giver knows that the money given has made a difference. Rather than contemplating one's shadows of doubt, one can stand in the shadows cast by the newly erected building built by mission funds and feel the difference that has been made in the local community. The rise in church cooperation and the decline in denominational loyalty has increased the passion for neighborhood socialized ministries while diminishing the thirst for mission efforts that one cannot see, touch, feel, or hear.

The movie *Sister Act* is a prime example of the impact that hands-on ministry can have on both the local community and on the participants in the church. Mother Superior, the diaconate, the presbytery, and the executive council may all be petrified at the thought of attempting this new trend, but the results can be striking.

Balancing Local and Global

I am in no way suggesting that foreign missions activities are no longer appropriate. But, for a time, it seemed as if foreign missions was the only mission game in town. The only mission game in town was actually out of town.

Churches need a balance between local and global missions—for several reasons. First, God commands churches to reach out to Jerusalem, Judea, Samaria, and to the remotest parts of the earth. America has too many resources not to share them with the entire world. It is just as great a sin to reach out only to one's immediate community as it is to reach out only across the seas. Second, the spiritual gift "mix" of a congregation may allow it to perform a ministry in another setting where the locals do not have those gifts or the training or resources available to accomplish the task; a great deal of ministry potential would be lost if churches abandoned global missions. Third, the excitement from one ministry often spawns another. A church might never consider a particular localized ministry until it catches the vision of what has been done in another setting. Conversely, a church may wish to work to replicate in another location a successful ministry piloted in the local parish.

Global mission must not be abandoned, but it must be altered. If possible, even global mission should be performed with a hands-on, local church mindset and approach. Denominations that send out foreign missionaries on behalf of local churches must ask, "How can the local churches build a stronger relationship with their foreign missionaries?" Denominations that do not accomplish this task will have fewer and fewer foreign missionaries to send because the trend in giving is to support only those causes with which one can readily identify.

Doing Hands-On Ministry

Many people have suggested that the twenty-first-century church will be more like the first-century church than the twentieth-century church. If this premise is true, it might be helpful to recall what the first-century local church was like. Howard Snyder makes several helpful observations to aid our recollections and predict the changes that would be necessary if we acted like a first-century church:

> Initially, all church buildings would have to be sold. The largest church could contain no more than 100 members. Congregations could rent public property as needed. Home Bible studies would be the norm rather than mid-week services on church property. All pastors would need to seek secular employment. . . . New churches would be started in the most economically disadvantaged, rather than the most economically advantaged, neighborhoods.[5]

That was the profile of the first-century church. Many of its characteristics might return in the next century.

Dietrich Bonhoeffer wrote, "The Church is the Church only when it exists for others."[6] It sometimes seems to me that some institutions exist for the wrong group of people. Many argue that schools exist for teachers rather than students. Some say that hospitals exist for doctors rather than patients and that service clubs primarily serve members rather than their communities.

Could it be that churches are beginning to break an unfortunate pattern of institutions believing that they exist for the wrong group of people? Could it be that churches are starting to realize that they exist for others rather than their members? I hope so. Those that wake up will still be churches fifty years from now. I'm afraid that those that don't will be fond memories in someone's scrapbook.

Callahan has promoted the concept of hands-on community ministry for quite some time. In a conference setting I listened to him parallel the church to a military MASH unit:

> Today's churches are similar to MASH units in the Korean War. They are faced with a shortage of supplies and a shortage of personnel. They are constantly faced with the delivery of competent services on the front lines.[7]

Callahan encourages all American churches to think of themselves as missionary churches, serving on the front lines . Too few resources for too many tasks? Try to think of your church as a spiritual MASH unit rather than as a well-funded service agency. The change of perspective will not add any more resources to a local congregation, but it can save your nerves.

You see, churches, like people, are less likely to complain about what they expect to find. Tension is reduced as the gap between expectations and reality is narrowed. When our children were at the ages of one and three, at the end of the day my wife often greeted me by relating several disasters du jour. After a while I kept track of the number of dilemmas that occurred each day—the median was three. I suggested that she might expect three daily disasters rather than treating each one as a surprise. (I was trying to help her ward off the high level of frustration that can accompany the task of raising children. I will admit, however, that my hands-on involvement proved to be more helpful than my calculations and philosophical advice.)

Statistical Support

Nearly everyone has felt the local effects of decreased governmental spending. Welfare programs, educational grants, and agricultural assistance have all been cut in recent years. These cuts also mean opportunities for ministry from local churches.

If the federal government places a greater percentage of the burden for health care costs on the shoulders of local communities, this move could have the greatest impact yet on local communities. Health care costs regularly consume 13 percent of the gross national product.

Crises, however, always imply opportunities. And opportunities abound for churches to promote holistic health for people in their communities. Granger Westberg, noted author and speaker, once called for churches to be viewed as environments for maintaining one's health. He cleverly exposed health care centers and hospitals as places for people to go once they have already become ill. Where do you go to maintain your health? Why not the church? I believe that all aspects of a person's health are connected. Church programs aimed at helping people reduce stress, manage time, control tempers, and develop better eating habits all can make a difference in the lives of people within their communities.

Loneliness is an additional area of potential community ministry for churches. The 1990 census reported that 12 percent of Americans now live alone, compared to 8 percent in the 1980 census.

In 1994 Americans spent an average of $93 million a day on lottery tickets. Every time an American buys a lottery ticket, the person purchases a piece of hope. Getting involved in one's church and community is also an investment of hope. Churches must somehow find a way to convince society of that fact.

Theoretical Support

If a church decides to get involved in hands-on ministry, then, theoretically speaking, the church must carefully select people to encourage this form of ministry. Hull describes the principle of selectivity in this way,

> Selectivity is the process of applying scriptural qualifications to the selection of leaders. Notice the target and purpose: the selection of leaders. The doctrine of selectivity does not apply to the general church populace in the same way that it does toward leaders.[8]

Hull suggests that local churches should recruit people to be leaders who exemplify the strongest set of characteristics espoused by Jesus and New Testament writers. A second theory espoused by many suggests that churches should go one step further: They should place their best leaders in the areas that are most important to them at any point in time. Combining these two theories suggests that local churches who wish to get involved in hands-on ministry should look seriously at encouraging their best leaders to lead the way in this type of ministry. This may mean freeing up people from existing positions.

Getting involved in hands-on ministry may also mean creating some "organizational slack" within your church. Do you currently have more positions to fill than you have active members? That is a real problem for churches that wish to do hands-on ministry. Opportunities to get involved in hands-on ministry often occur spontaneously rather than arising from a preconceived plan by a committee. A visit from the KKK may prompt a ministry aimed at improving ethnic relationships in your community. A shooting in your neighborhood may prompt a ministry to gang members. A school or legislative change may prompt a ministry to children. Someone may approach your church in midyear about joining a community organization such as Habitat for Humanity or Meals on Wheels. With no one available until next year, your church may miss out on an excellent hands-on ministry opportunity.

The theory of organizational slack suggests that organizations that wish to be responsive to their environment should not constantly push all of their personnel to the limit, lest, when an opportunity to respond does arise, no one is free to respond! If your congregation has more positions to fill than people available, it certainly has no organizational slack. Hull reports, "I had the gall to suggest that if we couldn't find the people to do the work, we leave vacancies."[9] Congregations should not fear vacancies. The ministries of Willow Creek Community Church, the second largest church in America, were built upon a "lead, not need" premise. Even when members complained of a lack of programming in certain areas, the congregation started no ministry until someone with the appropriate spiritual gifts came forward.

Helping members discover their spiritual gifts can also aid hands-on ministry. Simply the naming of certain spiritual gifts, such as mercy, evangelism, giving, helps, service, and craftsmanship, gives rise to possible community ministries.

It should be pointed out, however, that an emphasis on spiritual gifts can push a church too far into individualism and far away from cooperative hands-on ministry. Snyder warns that spiritual gifts should be viewed in light of community need, to ward off problems of competition:

The New Testament teaching about spiritual gifts is not a call for each Christian to "do his own thing" and forget the welfare of the group and the need of the world. Ministry is not determined exclusively by personal desire, but by the cross.[10]

Anecdotal Support

Stories related to successful ministries are numerous.

Erwin McManus started a community ministry in Texas reaching out to immigrants. He soon discovered that nearly everyone being ministered to was "illegal." So his ministry took a different turn. He taught them how to start their own church because, he warned them, "In six months, you're going to be deported." He now views the U.S. government as a missionary sending agency, sending newly trained missionaries back to their homeland![11]

Soon after Bruce Wall was called as pastor of an inner-city church in Dorcester, Massachusetts, he told Dorcester Temple that they would be responsible for ten blocks around the church. "Ten blocks would be drug, crime, and gang free . The residents would feel safe, the local police would be responsive, and the gangs would stay out."[12] On Friday nights, Bruce takes his "Spiritual Patrol and Prayer Walk" through his neighborhood's most crime plagued areas.

Bruce Wall is not the only pastor walking city streets—as a ministry. I have had the opportunity to walk the streets of Boston with Eugene Rivers during one of his weekly Friday night strides. He walks nearly as fast as he talks, at warp speed. He is a hands-on ministry kind of pastor. A Philadelphia gang member veteran, he carried his first gun at the age of fifteen and knows how to walk the walk and talk the talk of the streets. As we walked the streets together, I felt unbelievably safe in this former high-crime area of inner-city Boston. The safety was part fantasy and part reality. Someone was stabbed three blocks from where we paused to talk that night. Gene cannot understand why every other pastor in America is not attempting to do what he is doing. I grew up in the metropolitan area of Indianapolis. I could not do what Gene is doing. I did, however, experience a dramatic stirring in my soul, a burden to minister to the local community, that has not subsided since that walk with Gene on a Friday night last May at one in the morning.

Inner-city ministry is a tough ministry. Tony Evans laments,

What's true of physical leprosy is true of spiritual leprosy. We have
a generation of young people whose consciences have lost the ability to feel pain. . . . Unafraid of their parents, the police, or even
death, they can kill without feeling, rape without remorse, and rob
without concern for consequences.[13]

But not all churches are inner-city churches. Not all church-based
community ministry will take place in the inner-city. Your own successful ministry need not be so dramatic. Community ministries may be
started to meet the needs of pregnant teenagers, kids who have no place
to go after school, teens who do not feel loved, singles who have no
place to go on Saturday night, smokers who want to quit, divorced people who need support, jailed people who need visiting, and on and on.
Riverside Avenue Baptist Church in Muncie, Indiana, began a ministry
"to offer education and support to patients and caretakers of individuals
with Parkinson's disease." The First Baptist Church of Gresham, Ore-
gon, began program R.E.X. to "provide worship and social time for men-
tally disabled adults while raising the awareness that ALL belong to
God's family."

To begin hands-on ministry, the least of your worries will be finding
an appropriate place to begin.

Theological Support

It is much easier to thank God that we are not like our community than
to try to minister with our community. Consider the story of the Pharisee and the publican in Luke 18:9-17. Both the Pharisee and the publican were sinners. But the Pharisee believed that his sins were not as bad
as and could be atoned for more easily than the publican's.

The church always has had its top ten list of sins. That is unfortunate
because it entices the church into thinking that its sins are not as bad as
others', and it lures it into ministering only to people with similar kinds
of sins. Hands-on ministry will never be successful with such erroneous
presuppositions. A church that chooses not to minister to particular
people because their sin seems to be greater than their own is not fulfill-
ing the great commission of Jesus Christ.

The church always has been called to reach out to its community in precise, helpful ways. Matthew 25 provides a beautiful framework for understanding hands-on ministry. The chapter contains three stories that, when presented as a grouping, demonstrate a holistic approach to ministry. The first story, the parable of the ten maids with the lampstands, encourages the church always to be prepared. The second story, the parable of the talents, encourages the church to take risks. The third story, sometimes referred to as the judgment section, provides helpful criteria for judging the ministries of the church. This third story provides the content for ministry. "Whenever you did it for any of my people, no matter how unimportant they seemed, you did it for me" (Matt. 25:40 CEV). The church is called to be prepared. But preparation can lead to being overly cautious. Some congregations are so cautious that they would never risk losing some of their resources in order to produce results. What results? Feeding the hungry. Giving drink to the thirsty. Clothing the naked. Welcoming the stranger. Visiting the sick. Going to the prisoner. Ministries displayed in Matthew 25.

Jesus ministered to every group that had been disenfranchised by his society. Are we ministering to people with AIDS? Gang members? Alcoholics? Single parents? People in our society have great needs. Introducing them to Jesus Christ will not remove their struggles in life; it will introduce them to someone who can give them peace amidst their grappling.

Hands-on ministry was applauded by the prophets (Isa. 61:1-3) and was especially emphasized by Paul (see 2 Cor. 8:5; Gal. 6:9-10) and other New Testament writers.

Once Christians have received ministry in particular ways, they are called to minister to others in similar ways (2 Cor. 1:3-4). A divorced person may feel led to lead a divorce recovery group. Many recovering alcoholics have ministered to other alcoholics. Hands-on ministries may arise out of the experiences of your members. Although it is never appropriate for one person to say to another, "I know how you feel," people who have experienced particular crises are more in tune with the needs of others in similar circumstances. Clay Noah exhorts the church with these words:

> Mission begins by enabling people to minister. Begin with one thing and make it better. Then tackle something else. Love people

and they will love each other. Care about people in the ministries of the church and they will begin to care about one another.[14]

This megatrend for me is clearly a "should." Every church should be about the work of hands-on ministry.

Where We Begin

Discussing the Trend

1. Does your church have more positions to fill than people available? Invite members of your nominating committee to help answer this question.
2. When is the last time your church responded to a community need? How long did it take? What channels did you follow?
3. Is your church more concerned about being prepared and garnering its resources, or taking risks in order to produce ministry results? How can you achieve more of a balance between the two?
4. In what ways is your church currently:
    a. Feeding the hungry?
    b. Giving drink to the thirsty?
    c. Clothing the naked?
    d. Welcoming the stranger?
    e. Visiting the sick?
    f. Going to the prisoner?
    (Include both literal and figurative answers to these questions.)
5. How connected do you feel to your foreign missionaries? Your national missionaries? How can you get more connected? How can your denomination practice ministry overseas or nationally while giving local congregations a sense of hands-on ministry?
6. Shawchuck and Perry provide a set of questions (which I have paraphrased) for helping a church ponder hands-on ministry:[15]
    a. Why should your church reach out to its community?
    b. Why should your community be interested in your church?
    c. What currently inhibits your church from hands-on ministry?
    d. What church characteristics are important as a church seeks to reach out to its community?

e. Where are some places in your community that your church could minister to individuals?
f. Should you link with another church in a hands-on ministry?
g. Should you link with an agency in a hands-on ministry?
h. Are there any limits to your church's responsibility in this ministry?

Applying the Trend

1. Rent the video *Sister Act* for the group most responsible for ministry decisions in your church. Bring popcorn, cokes, and an open mind. Be sure to leave time for discussion following the movie.
2. Study the book *Basic Steps toward Community Ministry: Guidelines and Models in Action* by Carl S. Dudley, available from The Alban Institute.
3. Try to find out if your denomination has compiled a list of people or churches performing successful community ministries—a type of ministry bank. If so, get a copy of the list. Use the list to prompt ideas within your church and then invite people from other churches to make a presentation at your church. People love to talk about successful ministries even more than doing the ministries. (It's part of that old pattern of surrogate missions. So be careful not to take advantage of the people's time and be careful not to replace the performance of a ministry in your own church with the discussion of a ministry. It's easy to do!)
4. Contact your middle judicatory personnel for help in this area as needed.
5. A group of pastors and laity in Boston calls itself the Ten Point Coalition. They strive to serve their community in ten specific ways. If appropriate, consider serving your community in ways similar to theirs:
    a. Sponsor Adopt-a-Gang programs to organize and evangelize youth in gangs.
    b. Commission missionaries to serve as advocates for African-American and Latino juveniles in the courts.
    c. Commission youth evangelists to do street-level one-on-one evangelism with youth involved in drug trafficking.

d. Establish accountable community-based economic development projects that go beyond the rhetoric of political visions to generate actual revenue for local communities.

e. Establish links between suburban and downtown churches for inner-city ministry.

f. Initiate and support neighborhood crime-watch programs within local church neighborhoods.

g. Establish working relationships between local churches and community-based health centers to provide pastoral counseling for families during times of crisis.

h. Convene a working summit meeting for Christian African-American and Latino men to discuss the development of Christian brotherhoods that would provide rational alternatives to violent gang life.

i. Establish rape crisis drop-in centers and services for battered women in churches.

j. Develop an aggressive African-American and Latino history curriculum, with an additional focus on the struggles of women and poor people, to be taught in churches.

CHAPTER SIX

From Reasonable Spirituality to Mysterious Spirituality

America is experiencing a resurgence of interest in spirituality. At first glance, that sounds like a contradiction to an earlier statement that society and the church have been heading in separate directions. The apparent paradox is quickly solved with this explanation: Society is not disinterested in God; society is disinterested in the institutionalized church. Society has become increasingly distrustful of all institutions. Like it or not, most people still view the church as an institution. Moberg suggests that the church as a social institution includes "all organizations which directly seek to kindle, renew, and guide the religious life of people."[1] Society has not detached itself from spirituality; it is just rebelling against the ways that the church has sought to guide spiritual experiences. In what ways has the church failed to kindle, renew, and guide the religious lives of its people? The next section reveals the answers.

Where We've Been

The church has sought to guide the spiritual lives of its members in very practical, reasonable ways. That sounds like a compliment. It is not. Contrary to Western thought, spirituality is anything but reasonable and practical!

Ever since medieval times, the Western church has reacted against knowing God by direct experience and supported knowing God through secondary means, such as the Bible, sermons, devotional writings, theology, commentaries, and hymns. The church has encouraged people to reason about God more than it has encouraged them to relate to God.

Reasoning about God is helpful but limiting because it is impersonal. Communicating with God in a direct manner allows God to speak to our specific situation.

This historic tradition dates as far back as Aristotle, who suggested that humans receive knowledge from God only through their senses. Think of the implications of that. It limits access to God to the processes of hearing about God and reading about God. The other three senses of touch, taste, and smell made little sense in terms of getting to know God. Aristotle never expected God to self-reveal in a dream or a thought or a prayer what could be discovered through intellect and reason. Plato, who is often portrayed as Aristotle's counterpart, advocated for a direct route in encountering God. Plato did not discount sensory experience but suggested that human beings search for spiritual realities to help guide their understanding of the physical world.

In the battle between Aristotle and Plato, Aristotle won by a landslide. His victory is evidenced in writers that followed, including Comte, Frazer, Husserl, Heidegger, and Bultmann, who all sought to develop a philosophy of humankind that "would give the same certainty to its conclusions about human beings that physical science seemed to have given to chemistry and physics."[2] The basic assumptions for all fields of study in Western thought, including religion, came from facts and figures—or they were perceived to be invalid. Direct experiences with God, championed by Plato, were not to be trusted. Religion became firmly rooted in the outer physical world. The inner world of prayer, thought, and direct contact with God was viewed with great skepticism.

These trends continued in full force even through the nineteenth century:

> The positivistic scientists of the last century convinced most people that the only realities were things that could be explained in material terms and understood rationally. The theologians were no exception, so Christian theology went through a brainwashing from which it has only begun to recover.[3]

Spirituality, however, was never entirely lost during this age of reason. People like George Fox would not allow it. George Fox and his disciples in the Quaker Church promoted an acceptance of mysterious rather than reasonable spirituality. Fox suggested that God reveals pieces of information to people directly, apart from their senses. Apart from reason. "Call it a mystery, but I say it happens," people such as Fox claimed. Statements like this alarmed people. "How can you trust what you cannot read or audibly hear?" As is evidenced in the following passage by Robert Barclay, one of Fox's disciples, the promotion of this mysterious kind of spirituality was often attacked by those who continued to promote a more reasonable form of spirituality. Theologians had reached a point of trusting nothing other than scripture in terms of knowing God. Barclay battled this notion:

> Moreover, these divine inward revelations, which we make absolutely necessary for the building up of true faith, neither do nor can contradict the outward testimony of the Scriptures, or right and sound reason.[4]

Barclay contended that divine revelations and inward illuminations could be just as clear as scripture and the natural reasoning of humans.

A few others, but not many, followed Fox and Barclay's blazed trail. Beginning with the twentieth century, the Pentecostals rekindled a sense of mysterious spirituality among many people. For many years the church offered a monopoly on the Holy Spirit to the Quakers and the Pentecostals, and they gladly accepted. This is one primary reason for their growth in this century.

Did the Pentecostal movement renew people's interest in the Holy Spirit? Or did people already yearning for more emphasis on the Holy Spirit discover the Pentecostal movement? I don't know. It's a chicken and egg question. Naisbitt, who claims that followers create leaders, would probably argue for the latter.

In any case, the Pentecostal movement picked up many people starved for a fresh emphasis on the Holy Spirit. But not all of them. When the mainline churches ignored direct experiences with God for so long, along came many religious groups, sects, and cults eager to fill the void. The primary appeal of many of the newest religions today is an acute emphasis on mysterious spirituality. When people discovered that the leadership of the church was unwilling to, or uncomfortable with, talk about the Holy Spirit and the mysteries of God, they sought a deeper sense of spirituality elsewhere. Leaders unwilling to talk about the Holy Spirit propelled multitudes out of their churches to look elsewhere for their manna from heaven. Can the mainline churches ever feel comfortable again talking openly about mysterious religious experiences, direct experiences with God, and the Holy Spirit? I believe they can. In fact, that's where many of them are headed.

Where We're Headed

Reasonable spirituality involves encountering God through our senses. For a long time that was the only means that made sense to Western thinkers. But all that is beginning to change. People in America and the Western world are starting to encounter God directly, apart from their senses. Is God available that way? A lot of people, including scientists, are beginning to think so.

Receiving the Support of Scientists

For many people in America, spirituality is no longer espoused as reasonable but is accepted as mysterious. In fact, the entire universe is increasingly viewed by scientists with a sense of wonder rather than a sense of the ordinary.

> As Werner Heisenberg—one of the greatest of modern physicists— has put it, the natural language which speaks of things like God and soul probably comes much closer to stating the nature of reality than any of the exactly defined physical terms like mass and inertia.[5]

People are accepting a more mysterious view of spirituality because they have discovered that the world in which they live is more mysterious and unexplainable than once thought. It is ironic that for many years theologians tried to emulate scientists with their precise methodologies built upon the factual and logical portions of scripture, only to discover that in the height of such scientific emulation, science was turning back toward mystery.

Quantum physics no longer allows scientists to claim to the rest of the world that anything that cannot be seen or measured does not exist:

Quantum physics challenges those who so assume the complete
knowledge of reality by physical science. Contemporary physics . . .
has learned that there are occurrences of the physical world which
appear so completely to escape comprehension that these occurrences can be described neither by the conventional scientific understandings of the physical world nor by contemporary physics.[6]

Scientists no longer believe that everything in the world can be
measured. They no longer believe that every action has a reaction. They
no longer believe that they can observe the smallest particles of the universe without influencing the behavior of those particles simply by the
observation. In fact, they no longer believe that the universe is com-
posed solely of particles. Waves, force fields, and other phenomena have
become just as real as particles. Scientists now believe that we live in a
universe whose space is curved: limited, but without boundaries. They
no longer believe in absolute time; time can be measured only in relationship to place, motion, and light. This new understanding of the universe does not merely leave room for God. It goes way beyond that. It
makes it impossible to understand the world apart from some other unexplainable outside force or influence upon the earth. Those who claim
that God does not exist will have to come up with some other explanation of this outside force.

The world of science has shifted from being one of the greatest
underminers of religious experience to being one of its greatest support-
ers! Based on the contributions of quantum physics, the world's scientists are quickly becoming major proponents of mysterious spirituality!
In previous years, scientists had all but convinced many that any activity
that could not be seen and measured did not exist.

Explaining the Spiritual World

Where is this unexplainable force that exerts its influence on our natural
world? It is contained in a spiritual world alongside our natural world.
God exists in this spirit world, along with angels, demons, and the devil.
Humans exist in the natural world of space, time, and matter. Kelsey
believes that the soul or psyche of an individual is the part of every human that connects that human with the spiritual world. Have you ever

known the phone would ring before it rang? Have you ever known who would be on the other end of the line before the person spoke? Have you known that something good or bad had happened to a friend of yours even before you received the news? Have you ever had a dream that gave you knowledge that you otherwise would not have had? Have you ever awakened from a sound sleep with an answer to a problem? Believing in a spiritual world alongside our physical world helps explain these experiences. At times, all humans receive information and experience things apart from their senses.

Kelsey believes that two separate worlds exist side by side. Lest one expect to hear the voice of Rod Serling detailing another episode of "The Twilight Zone," let me suggest that Kelsey's model is quite practical in explaining many theological beliefs that would be otherwise unexplainable. To me, Kelsey's model helps explain the incarnation of Christ, the Trinity, being filled of the Holy Spirit, the interpretation of dreams, and the continual influence of demons. Kelsey developed this model using data from counseling sessions. So many clients told of experiences that could not be explained using a model of only the natural world that Kelsey developed this model to help make sense of the real-life experiences of his clients who described contact with the spiritual world.

The other day in Bible study, our group was studying 1 Samuel 28, where Saul seeks the help of a medium to talk to the dead and departed Samuel. The conventional model, which views heaven and hell as a place sealed off from the rest of society, is inadequate in explaining what happened to enable Samuel to communicate with Saul. The conventional model raises questions such as, "Is Samuel a ghost? Why wasn't Samuel in heaven yet? Did God give Samuel special permission to be released from heaven to speak to Saul?" Kelsey's model conjures up no such questions because it depicts a spiritual world alongside our natural world. Samuel communicated to Saul by crossing the boundary separating the natural world from the spiritual world.

Commencing the Journey

Reasonable spirituality is quickly becoming as outdated as Aristotle's other views—that Earth was the center of the universe and that heavenly bodies maintained a physical existence somewhere above Earth. Today the number of people clamoring for an openness to the mysteries of God can no longer be handled through a small proportion of the churches in America. The mainline churches must acknowledge the mysterious pathways to God and encourage people to come aboard for the journey.

Just what does this new journey entail? The answer depends on whether you are inquiring as a church leader trying to bring about change in your congregation or as an intrigued individual wishing to embark on a personal journey of discovery.

If you are a church leader who bears some responsibility for the spiritual vitality of your congregation, the first step is to present God as approachable and yet to be discovered. Never discount the authority of scripture, but promote the idea that there is more to God than dissecting scripture and taking sermon notes. Some church leaders have unknowingly presented their view of God as the only view. Others have done it on purpose. Wicks asserts, "We mistake our image of God and the gifts of God for the true undefinable God."[7] People must be allowed to pursue their mysterious spiritual experiences and be given permission to share them with the church body.

A second step involves fostering the idea that scripture supports direct contact with God. "For Western Christian people there is probably no better way to effect this change than to take the New Testament itself, in its entirety, very seriously."[8] The Bible presents numerous stories of visions, dreams, healings, encounters, and insights from God.

Reflect upon your corporate worship experiences. What parts of your worship services encourage people to encounter God? Are you presenting multiple opportunities and multiple methods for encountering God? If you had received word that God had a specific message for your congregation this Sunday, would that alter the plan for your worship?

What materials and suggestions has your church offered for people to experience God? On a continuum that views God as totally practical on one end and totally mysterious on the other, where do you fall? Do your public statements match this answer? Have you offered personal examples of your own mysterious or mystical experiences with God?

For the individual seeking to encounter God personally, the methods of approaching God in mysterious ways, as opposed to approaching God through one's senses, are numerous. A few guidelines, coupled with a permissive imagination, may help.

Discovering the mysteries of God is not an easy task, "For the gate is narrow and the road is hard that leads to life, and there are few who find it" (Matt. 7:14). The first guideline for someone wishing to encounter God directly—to begin to unlock the mysteries—is to initiate the task with determination. Know that you will experience setbacks and frustrations along the way. Begin your journey with the awareness that you are taking up a task that will not be easy.

This first guideline gives rise to the second, reflection. The traveler along this road must have some way to chart progress, lest the progress be lost in the prolonged process of encounter. Find some means of reflecting upon what you learn about God. This may be done in a number of ways, including journal writing, talking with another person about your progress, or quietly meditating at regular intervals along the way.

A third guideline is "experiment." There is no single pathway to encountering God directly. Different methods work for different people. Determination, reflection, and experimentation are three keys to unlocking the mysteries of direct experience with God.

Beyond these universal guidelines, there are several specific means of exploring God. Prayer is a must. There are many other ways to experience God, but for someone wishing to encounter God more fully, prayer is the place to start. Combining prayer with meditation and silence is even more beneficial. Many people set aside times of silence. Others record their dreams. Keep a pencil and paper or a small tape recorder beside your bed and get your dreams down before you get up, or you will never remember them. I have introduced many youth to fasting through World Vision's "Let It Growl program." Fasting is an excellent method of encountering God for those whose chemistries allow it. Some people "journal" to make progress in their search to encounter God directly. Contemplating scripture, rather than analyzing scripture, can also help. Allow scripture to speak to you in a new way. Finally, some people choose to enlist the help of a spiritual "director," mentor, or guide, to serve as a catalyst for their thoughts.

Statistical Support

Seventy-three percent of Americans report that having a close personal relationship with God is something they greatly desire for the future. Only 50 percent of Americans state that being a part of a church is something that they greatly desire for the future.[9] Society is not disinterested in God, they are disinterested in the institutional church.

One of the reasons for this may be that the institutional church has not encouraged people to express their spirituality. Fifteen hundred American adults were asked the question, "Have you ever had the feeling of being very close to a powerful spiritual force that seemed to lift you out of yourself?"[10] Forty percent answered yes. Of those, 50 percent said "several times" and 12 percent said "often." Sixty-seven percent of those responding yes rated their experience at the very top of a seven-point intensity scale.

From the above survey, would you expect more of the people responding yes to be male or female? Protestant or Catholic? College-educated? Statistically speaking, those responding yes were disproportionately male, college-educated, and Protestant.

Americans are encountering God. Many would like to talk about their experiences with a friend or with a pastor. Some are getting that opportunity. Many are not. Many Americans are experiencing a spiritual hungering for the presence of God. Many will look until they find a place where others are having a similar hunger satisfied. Then they will stop looking and begin experiencing God in the company of friends.

Theoretical Support

Don Cupitt suggests that the age-old human reliance on reason and logic provided a false sense of security.[11] Breaking with reason and order, he claims that there was only a false, not true, sense of confidence in reason. Where he heads in his book *Radicals and the Future of the Church* is more akin to gnosticism than Christianity, and thus takes an entirely different direction from this book. Cupitt turns everything over to one's experience, "You have to see yourself as being all on the surface, the sum of your own external relations . . . people have no insides."[12] Cupitt is one of a growing number of people who lift up the importance of perception in gauging reality.

In terms of theoretical support for encountering God directly, he makes a strong case that the open lines between the mind and the spirit world have replaced a total reliance upon reason and the senses. The world no longer believes that it must touch, smell, taste, hear, and see things in order for them to be there.

Where I break with Cupitt and other authors can be explained via the classic analogy of the blind people and the elephant. As the story goes, several were asked to touch an elephant and describe what they experienced. The first, touching the side of the elephant, described it as a barn. The second, touching the leg of the elephant, described it as a column. The third, touching the trunk of the elephant, described it as a branch.

Based upon this example, many have suggested that what one perceives is reality. In essence, they suggest that there really is no elephant. If one perceives that she is touching a barn, she is. If another perceives that he is touching a tree, he is touching a tree. Those who suggest that there is no real elephant do not advocate for a continuing search for the elephant; they cease the search for truth.

While I respect people's right to define the realities of life, God, and even truth in their own minds and terms, I am not ready to give up the elephant. Peoples' perceptions may be the most real thing to them, and I defend each person's right to hold personal views. I still, however, believe that there are universal truths, and a universal God, to be discovered individually by each person.

I promote Western meditation as opposed to Eastern meditation. The goal of Western meditation is to encounter God more fully. The goal of Eastern meditation is to lose oneself in God. I believe that Eastern meditation is dangerous. Whenever I encounter God directly, I can expect those perceptions of God to be consistent with my other understandings of God. My new understandings may expand, redirect, or even transform my previous understandings, but learnings gained from direct experiences with God should not directly contradict learnings gleaned from scripture and reason. Learning about God is a continuous process of filtering both my direct experiences and the experiences of my senses through the lens of previous experiences.

I add the warning that the promotion of mysterious spirituality can lead down a dangerous path—the path of contradictory understanding of God among Christians. Mysterious spirituality encourages each person to try to discover the mysteries of God according to his or her own unique path. S o if your understanding of God differs from my understanding of God, then I cannot question your outcome, so long as your intent was to freely discover God rather than try to prooftext predisposed suppositions. If you are convinced that your motives of discovering God were as pure as mine, then I have no right to question anything.

But just because two people hold contradictory views of God doesn't mean that the search has ended or that the two views will never get any closer. As each person continues to pursue the real elephant, the essence of who God is, then both people must be open to the continual altering of their understanding of God. Two searches based upon scripture, dialogue, theology, and now, direct experiences with God, should theoretically intersect, given enough time for the journeys to mature. Yes, there are risks, but isn't the potential outcome of knowing God more fully worth that risk?

Anecdotal Support

I was introduced to the topic of encountering God directly through a course in seminary titled Transpersonal Psychology and the Spiritual Life. That is quite a title! It was quite a course! The instructor guided us in meditation for the first ten minutes of every class. Every class! The course met three times a week for sixteen weeks. As a result of those experiences, to this day, I can pause in the middle of the day and focus on God and begin to relate to God in a direct manner. For me meditation is a means of relating to or encountering God more fully.

I understand that not everyone will have the same desire to relate to God in this way. But, for those who do, the church needs to encourage the opportunities. I try to present God as mysterious and yet approachable, awesome and yet able to connect to people in real ways. Periodically people express an interest in getting closer to God. Accepting invitations from a Sunday school class, a Bible study group, and individual church members, I have taught people how to meditate. Other people have some mystical experience they cannot understand, but which they have a need to discuss and which often pulls them into a journey of encountering God. I think every congregation has people who undergo mystical experiences. But not every congregational leader gives permission for them to be shared.

A few summers ago I led a male spirituality class in our church. We studied Robert Bly's *Iron John*.[13] The book depicts various stages of male development. I supplemented our discussions with notes and theories regarding spirituality. Each participant seemed to appreciate the class and the opportunities to explore God and male development issues simultaneously. I discovered that each member of the class, without exception, had experienced direct encounters with God that served to adjust not only his personal life, but his view of God.

Theological Support

Mysterious spirituality is entirely biblical. Kelsey relates that there are five types of spiritual experiences in the New Testament: (1) direct actions of God, including healings and miracles; (2) indirect revelations, which include dreams, visions, and inward hearing; (3) intuitive discernment, which includes deciding whether an influence is of God or Satan; (4) direct knowledge from God apart from the senses; (5) direct possession, which includes prophecies and speaking in tongues. Kelsey reports that 3,874 of the 7,957 verses in the New Testament contain one of these five experiences of the Spirit.[14] It is apparent that the people who lived in New Testament times did not ignore the Holy Spirit. The Spirit was an integral part of their lives. As one begins to examine the scriptures, it is apparent that New Testament Christians encountered God directly.

They also encountered God corporately. Whenever the church gathered for worship, the participants expected the Spirit to take the lead. The word church is derived from the New Testament Greek word *ekklesia*, which literally means a "meeting," without any reference to purpose or organization. When we think of "meeting" today, we often picture two or more people encountering one another. But it seems that the New Testament word for church suggested a meeting between the people and God, rather than one another. Viewing church as an opportunity to encounter God is much more powerful than many of our images of church today. "The rock which Jesus had in mind was something infinitely stronger than any human organization can be."[15] Viewing the church as more of an organization than a place to interact with the Spirit of God misses the mark. When the people of God, gathered as the church, fail to encounter God, then they are not really the church.

The New Testament is filled with examples of people encountering God directly. Grant, Thompson, and Clarke reveal how Paul emphasized direct experiences with God:

> It is remarkable . . . how much the language of Paul is filled with
> terms which express the presence of divine force, power and energy

in the world through the sending of the Spirit by the risen Jesus (I
Cor 1:18,24; 2:4-5; Eph 1:15-23; Phil 2:12-13).

These authors add, "The spiritual task . . . is to find ways in which
the immense psychic resources of our humanity can be disclosed and set
free to be the carriers of the very power of God at work in our midst."[16]
Many people experience the direct presence of God on a regular basis—
because God wants to encounter us as much as we seek to encounter
God. This pathway of approaching God directly is mysterious because it
is not accomplished through our senses, not because God does not desire
it to take place. God wants us to discover the mysteries of the kingdom.
  Sanford points this out in his analysis of two parables of the kingdom of God, found side by side in Matthew 13.

> The kingdom of heaven is like treasure hidden in a field, which
> someone found and hid; then in his joy he goes and sells all that he
> has and buys that field. Again, the kingdom of heaven is like a mer-
> chant in search of fine pearls; on finding one pearl of great value, he
> went and sold all that he had and bought it (Matt. 13:44-46).

In the first parable the kingdom of God is likened to an object. We, as
human beings, search for the kingdom of God. In the following verses,
the kingdom of God is likened to an individual rather than an object. Not
only are we, as individuals, searching for God, but God is searching for
us! If the second parable had an identical meaning to the first, the kingdom of God would have been the pearls, but it was not.

> So, the paradox is that the kingdom is both that which we find with-
> in ourselves as an inner treasure and also that which is searching to
> find us. . . . We are the fine pearls if the kingdom can take root
> within us.[17]

God wants to be available. We can read about God. We can listen
to others talk about God. And recently more of us have begun to see that
we can encounter God directly, mysteriously, unexplainably, apart from
our senses. That is where many in the church are headed: from reasonable encounters with God to mysterious encounters with God. Are we
ready for this trend? We may not be. God, however, is ready, and that

may be all that is necessary for this megatrend to become the dominating approach toward spirituality in our churches.

Where We Begin

Discussing the Trend

1. How does your congregation encourage people to encounter God?
2. Do you think that God still relates to us through dreams and visions, or is that a lot of hocus pocus?
3. Does your congregation more often promote reasonable spirituality or mysterious spirituality?
4. Have you ever had a mystical experience? What was its intensity?
5. What specific ways can you list that your church has encouraged people to tell of their experiences with God?
6. Imagine that the Bible is no longer available to you. How would you expect to receive input from God? How would you attempt to communicate with God? Do you think that the availability of scripture influences your efforts of direct communication with God? Is the Bible currently your sole source or one source among many of receiving information from God?

Applying the Trend

1. Study a book on spirituality, prayer, or Christian meditation with a group. Check the bibliography for examples.
2. Encourage your pastor to preach a series on the spiritual disciplines.
3. Sponsor a day of prayer in your church or a cluster of churches.
4. The next time you pray, say everything you can think of to tell God, then listen for the same amount of time.
5. Set aside thirty minutes a day and simply listen to God.
6. An analysis of the Myers-Briggs Type Indicator (MBTI) personality inventory can assist individuals in encountering God. For further information contact The Center for Applications of Psychological Type (CAPT), 2815 NW Thirteenth Street, Suite 401, Gainesville, FL 32609-2861. The Alban Institute has published several excellent

resources relating personality type to spirituality, including *Spiritual Awakening* by John Ackerman (using the MBTI) and *Discover Your Spiritual Type: A Guide to Individual and Congregational Growth* by Corinne Ware (using Urban T. Holmes's spiritual typology). Ware's book contains a description of the *lectio divina* method of devotional Bible reading, a method that has been a great resource for me.

7. Keep a journal of your experiences with God. Be sure to include your reflections and any insights received during times of meditation or silence.

8. Fast. Consult your physician before doing so. Find someone in your church who practices this discipline and seek that person's advice.

CHAPTER SEVEN

From Official Leadership to Gifted Leadership

What office a person holds in the church does not matter nearly as much as it once did. The days of churches turning all of the leadership tasks over to people who hold certain offices in the church are fading away.

What is replacing this outdated model of "official" leadership? Gifts. Churches are looking to people who are gifted in particular areas to lead those ministries in the church. The offices of bishop, elder, and deacon sound terribly biblical. So biblical that someone might wonder if this traditional style of ministry could ever yield to any other view. But it is happening. And the new model is just as biblical as the offices of the church. Spiritual gifts have ushered in a new era of church leadership. Churches are altering their approaches toward leadership issues.

Where We've Been

There was a time when a local church pastor was among the most respected and educated people within a community. The pastor seemed to know all of the community movers and shakers by name. For good reason. The pastor was one of the movers and shakers. Society held a high regard for the pastoral office. The pastor received a lot of privileges in town, not just from parishioners. Everyone wanted to get on the good side of the local pastor.

That is hard to give up. For many, there will be no choice. It will be taken away.

There are still places in America where the local pastor is one of the most respected people in town, regardless of personality. But the trend is for society to become increasingly intolerant and less respectful of the church and its leadership. More and more, a church and its leadership gain respect within a community by meeting the needs of people within that community, not by virtue of their official status. The power of the church is shifting from legitimate power and coercive power to referent power and expert power. Churches are becoming respected more for what community and social needs they can meet in the future than for their historic community standing. Communities are no longer yielding to churches simply because of their prominent status in the community. Communities are, however, often calling upon churches to assist them when the community has recognized the expertise of particular church members.

The shift between church and society is but the tip of the leadership iceberg. There are much larger leadership changes occurring within the institutionalized church than between the church and society. The title reverend once garnered a great deal of respect within the community and broader society. Multiply that respect by ten, and you have an accurate description of the relationship between a pastor and the laity of a local church. That, too, is changing.

Not all churches are ready for this storm brewing in church leadership. Neither pastors nor laity. It's hard to stop a storm from coming. Especially one that has been gaining strength since the sixteenth century.

Martin Luther was among the first and most vocal to complain about the level of power exhibited by the leadership of the church:

> The Romanists have, with great adroitness, drawn three walls round themselves, with which they have hitherto protected themselves, so that no one could reform them, whereby all Christendom has suffered terribly. First, if pressed by the temporal power, they have affirmed that the temporal power has no authority over them. . . . Secondly, if it were proposed to admonish them with Scriptures, they objected that no one may interpret the Scriptures but the Pope. Thirdly, if they are threatened with a council, they invented the notion that no one may call a council but the Pope.[1]

No wonder Martin Luther had more than a little difficulty with the Roman Catholic Church. This style of argument was at the heart of many of Luther's criticisms. Luther was more concerned about the lack of available dialogue between the church body and its leadership than he was about any one substantive issue. True dialogue could have brought about many of the changes that Luther supported. But in the sixteenth century, and in many twentieth-century churches, true dialogue between a church and its leadership does not take place.

In the formation of Protestantism did Luther get his wish for true dialogue between the church and its leadership? No. As is the case with many reforms, those who build the new system do not create a new system much different from the old.

Many churches broke with the Catholic Church only to erect three new walls of their own: (1) the wall that suggests that only pastors can handle the most sacred and holy elements in the church; (2) the wall that suggests that only pastors can deliver the final word on any word contained in scripture; (3) the wall that suggests that only pastors can do real ministry.

All these years we thought the storm had subsided between the church and its leadership. On the contrary, the stirrings within the church were merely gaining strength for complete leadership reformation the second time around.

Many pastors have put forth the notions that only they can deliver sermons, counsel people on spiritual issues, discuss death, deliver eulogies, baptize, hand out the bread and the cup, pray for the ill, visit the sick, wash feet, or moderate a church meeting. Some of the laity are beginning to question why.

Some have talked the talk that pastors are to be equippers of the saints, but have not chosen to walk the walk in very many areas of ministry. In the future, I believe we will all walk the walk. Yes, there are much greater shake-ups coming within the church walls than outside the church walls with regard to leadership.

Callahan refers to the brewing storm as the decline of the era of the professional minister. Prior to World War II pastors referred to their vocations. Since World War II they have referred to themselves as professionals. Professional implies that only those with extensive training can perform the specified tasks at hand. Imagine announcing that you will be performing your own child's appendectomy because you have recently read a book on surgery or had the opportunity to witness a similar operation. "Leave that to the professionals!" the community would clamor in unison. Only the health care professionals should

perform surgery. Only the ministry professionals should do ministry?!
Professionals are viewed as performing tasks that no one else would dare
perform without the correct set of credentials. "Today," Callahan declares, "the day of the professional minister is over. The day of missionary pastor has come."[2]

Callahan writes convincingly about this concept of the death of the
professional minister. One can sense that he has quickly shifted from
preaching to meddling when he writes,

> As pastors discovered they were no longer placed on a pedestal by
> the culture, they sought to regain the pedestal through the credentials
> of professionalism. *We went from pedestal to professional.*[3]

Callahan explains how the church decided that a master's degree
was essential to ministry and later how a doctoral degree was thought to
enhance ministry. I must admit that I am one with advanced degrees.
But I have always advocated for the ordination or full acceptance of
pastoral leadership apart from the required seven years of higher education required in my denomination and several others. I used my degrees
to focus the kind of continuing education courses I would have taken all
along, not to credential my words. At least, that's my rationalization!

Callahan explains how the focus of the professional minister is inside the church and how the focus of ministry for today's churches must
be outside the church.[4] So the days of the professional minister must
draw to a close if the church is going to survive. It is not a matter of ego.
It is a matter of ministry. The most effective means of ministry for today's churches is for all of the personnel of the church to get involved,
clergy and laity, in ministry together. The congregation that seeks to
employ one professional to do ministry on its behalf will not make it into
the next century. Likewise, the pastor who seeks to be called to a church
as the lone professional minister will not have a place to serve in the next
century.

In the past the church has promoted a double standard for doing
ministry. Still not convinced that the pastor was seen as the more important person in the hierarchy of church leadership? Just look at all of
the professions that use the term laymen: educators versus laymen, doctors versus laymen, clergy versus laymen, attorneys versus laymen. "Let
me put it in layman's terms for you," one says when simplifying the

language. It is impossible to discuss being a layperson and not feel
second class in the church. "There was nothing there now except a
single Commandment," Orwell writes in his book *Animal Farm*.
    It ran:

ALL ANIMALS ARE EQUAL
BUT SOME ANIMALS ARE MORE EQUAL THAN OTHERS.[5]

All church members are equal. But in the past some were more
equal than others. New days are coming. Leadership in the church is
changing. Naisbitt writes,

> The sun gets largest just before it goes under. Remember the bron-
> tosaurus? The brontosaurus got so huge just before its demise that it
> had to stay in the water to remain upright.[6]

Naisbitt originally wrote these words about labor unions. Somehow, I
think there is a message in these words for the professional minister.
New days are coming. Better days, in my mind.

Where We're Headed

Churches are using the spiritual gifts of their members in a variety of
ways. Some churches are using spiritual gift inventories of their members to nominate people to church offices. Other churches encourage
people with particular gifts to begin ministries related to their gifts without ever asking those people to hold a particular elected office in the
church. Denominations are paying close attention to spiritual gifts in
their searches for pastors of new mission congregations.
    This new style of leadership is based as much on the tone of gifts as
it is upon the physical and spiritual attributes themselves. Even without
handing out surveys, churches are relying more on the gifts of leaders,
wherever they may be in the church, rather than on the job descriptions
of particular officers or board members.
    A reader might critique the supposed newness of the spiritual gifts
concept. "Hasn't this concept of spiritual gifts been making a comeback
for most of this century?" Yes, it has. Spiritual gifts are not a new

emphasis. But the depth to which churches are incorporating this style of leadership is new. In the past many churches encouraged members to discover their spiritual gifts and then went on with business as usual. Today churches are beginning to incorporate brand new models of leadership based upon the giftedness of their members.

Here's the big change: When a new idea for ministry arises, churches are no longer thinking in terms of which church officer or board could best carry this out; they are thinking in terms of which person or team of people could best carry this out. People first; offices second. Churches are looking at gifts first and positions later, if at all. In some cases churches are combining both gifts and positions in ministry tasks. Some churches activate the creative channels of their church in the formulation of a ministry and later mobilize the official or positional channels to fund the ministry.

This new way of promoting leadership affects all of the relationships within the church—the relationships between church boards and other members, between church officers and ministry team leaders, and especially the relationships between clergy and laity.

Gifts leadership focuses upon people rather than positions. This focus breaks down the hierarchies of more traditional models of leadership. Relationships throughout the institutional church are changing rapidly. None of these changes are occurring more rapidly than the relationships between clergy and laity.

Breaking Down the Walls between Clergy and Laity

The most clear indication of a change in church leadership can be witnessed from laity and clergy interaction. Church involvement by the laity increased in emphasis in the 1950s. Since that time some churches have merely "tolerated" an increased emphasis on the part of the laity in ministry. Other churches, seeing the potential benefits to both laity and clergy, have praised this new trend. Many of the churches that have broad appeal today are those that do more than tolerate the augmented role of the laity. They nurture the new role of the liberated laity and shun the more traditional "Lone Ranger" pastor approach.

Everywhere you turn the laity is becoming more integrally involved in the life of the church. Laypeople are attending continuing education events, leading ministries, forming ecumenical partnerships, and even preaching sermons.

The laity is no longer a part of the audience, either in the worship service or the arenas for ministry. The laity is becoming increasingly involved in the lifeblood of the church. But this does not mean that there are no longer any distinctions between clergy and laity, even in congregations where laypeople are integrally involved. Hahn explains, "In the open church, clergy and laity have different roles, which are related to each other functionally, not hierarchically."[7] In previous years the differences between clergy and laity could often be explained via the professional minister model explained in the previous section. Today the distinct roles of clergy and laity have been altered in content. In some congregations the pastors are the equippers of ministers and the laity are the ministers. In other congregations the pastor serves as a kind of chaplain to the various boards and ministries. In still other congregational settings, the pastors appear to function in the areas of conflict and crisis, while the laity carries out the more routine ministries.

Some would argue that even though the content of the roles might change, there should always be clear lines between clergy and laity. I am not so sure. I can find very little support for the distinct roles of clergy and laity biblically, practically, or even in terms of effectiveness. The main argument I see for maintaining the clear lines relates to history and tradition. This first wave of change seems to involve altering the content but maintaining the distinction between clergy and laity. The second wave may involve a crumbling of all lines between clergy and laity.

One of the items that serves to maintain the clergy/laity distinction is ordination and all of the requirements it entails. But even this is changing. Anderson suggests, "There is less concern over degrees, accreditation, ordination, and other credentials, but an increased asking of the practical question, 'Can he or she do the job?'"[8] Anderson predicts that seminaries will move toward training either practical pastors or research theologians. If that happens, the preparation that pastors receive may prepare them more to be colleagues and partners with laity rather than merely educators and priests for laity.

Breaking Down the Walls between Churches and Denominations

Walls are crumbling not just between clergy and laity, but in other areas
of the church as well. Denominations are asking what they can do to
enhance the ministry of the local church rather than seeking to perform
ministry on the local church's behalf. Many denominations are helping
churches with start-up ministries in their local communities, helping
them plant new churches, providing tools for community-based needs
assessment, and contracting with churches ripe for moving toward the
next level of reaching their ministry potential.

Technology is one factor helping to break down the walls between
churches and their denominations.

> When large organizations are linked with computer networks and e-
> mail, they evolve "web like structures" in which information flows
> sideways, far different from the traditional pyramid-style hierarchy,
> where information moves mostly up and down.[9]

Increasingly denominations are discovering ways to link with their congregants via advanced technology.

Breaking Down the Walls between Men and Women

Naisbitt claims that the new corporate archetype is more female than
male.[10] For years churches have had feminine backbones. Now feminin-
ity is starting to pervade other parts of the body of Christ as well.
Rightly so.

The seminary I attended recently released a statement reaffirming
their stance that women are not called to preach. Two weeks after that
statement, they held their annual anonymous sermon-writing contest.
Guess the gender of the top three winners. That's right, all female!

I am proud that I currently serve in a denomination that in 1922
elected the first woman president of any denomination, Helen Barrett
Montgomery. It has always seemed strange to me that an institution like
the church, which has as its mandate releasing the prisoners and freeing
the oppressed, has consistently lagged behind society in affirming the
gifts of all of society. The support of women in ministry is a current
trend that is long overdue.

Other Walls

It seems that everywhere you turn to look within the institutional church, walls are crumbling. Episcopal churches are working with Lutheran churches. Catholic congregants are working with Methodists. Local churches are working with community agencies. As society becomes more indifferent toward the church, all of the parts of the church will find new ways to cooperate with one another.

The New Leadership

Will this new model of leadership require a new type of leader? Definitely. It will require leaders with strong, healthy egos who are able to work as partners with all of God's people. Note a difference between leaders with strong healthy egos and strong leaders. Naisbitt writes,

> strong leadership is anathema to a democracy . . . our government has not attracted strong leaders except in times of crisis. . . . In a crisis we choose Lincoln and FDR. In between we choose what's-his-name.[11]

I believe that this particular crisis, however, will be one driven not by strong leaders but by strong partnerships. People who need to be stroked by others, people who always need to be in charge, people who never admit that someone else can do a job better, people who can function only according to well-defined rules need not apply as leaders of tomorrow's churches.

> A leader is best when people barely know he exists. Not so good when people obey and acclaim him. Worse when they despise him . . . . when [a good leader's] work is done, his aim is fulfilled, they will say, "We did it ourselves."[12]

Today's church leaders should be able to work with others in a team approach. Though there may be times when pastors are still the experts, it will be imperative that they treat others with respect and value their gifts. They need to exercise what Bennis terms the "Pygmalian effect:

The difference between a lady and a flower girl is not how she behaves but how she is treated."[13]

Today's church leaders should also be synergistic.

> Synergy is the state in which the whole is more than the sum of the parts. Principle-centered people are synergistic. They are change catalysts. They improve almost any situation they get into. They work as smart as they work hard. They are amazingly productive, but in new and creative ways.[14]

Statistical Support

> Within the next few years, many of the churches that now have full-time pastors will have part-time pastors.

> Our church income is remaining constant, but our expenses continue to rise.

> There simply aren't enough priests for our parishes.

> Only a small percentage of our churches have been willing to call women pastors, and yet nearly half of our seminarians are women.

Everywhere people are lamenting conditions that will affect church leadership. "A recent survey by the National Opinion Research Center in Chicago reported that 94 percent of Catholic boys between the ages of fourteen and adulthood had never thought about the priesthood for themselves."[15] My own denomination recently began promoting a Church Vocations Sunday due to the lack of people entering our seminaries.

> Every study that has been made to analyze what makes churches grow points to the same thing—the quality and effectiveness of pastoral leadership. To make a comeback, mainline denominations simply must recruit and train a more effective clergy.[16]

All of the trends point toward the need for new leaders and new models of leadership.

It may be women who lead us into new models of church leadership. Every year the percentage of women starting small businesses continues to rise. Women are now starting their own businesses at twice the rate of men.[17] Naisbitt suggests this is happening largely because women have been barred from the boardrooms for so long. "No wonder so many talented, successful women said, 'The heck with this,' and started their own businesses."[18] In the days ahead women looking for nontraditional places to do ministry and churches looking for nontraditional approaches may find each other.

Theoretical Support

Several business and organizational theory concepts support the shift from official leadership to gifted leadership. These concepts include networking, entrepreneurship, intrapreneurship, and self-management.

Networking involves forming connections among teams of people within an organization. Many churches, denominations, and clusters of churches have successfully implemented what the business world would term networking. Within a cluster of churches in my denomination, I helped design a survey that polled churches to discover ministries in which they had experience or needed help. The task of connecting a church that had a desire to start a new ministry with another church that had already successfully implemented that ministry was easy; we simply linked churches in our area by compiling the data on a spreadsheet and disseminating it.

When it comes to responding to needs within an organization, networking responds much more quickly than more traditional approaches. The old model of official leadership would have waited for a church to express a need for ministry help to the appropriate regional or national denominational office. The denomination would then have sent out a denominational expert to help the church launch that particular ministry. If no one on staff already possessed that expertise, the staff minister in the appropriate office would have been commissioned to attend a continuing education event to gain the expertise needed or the office might have just responded, "We don't do that."

In many ways the old style of official leadership was effective. But it was also time consuming and hierarchical, two qualities that do not fit today's churches. "The shift from hierarchies to networking means that it matters less who your boss is, more how well you make the right connections with a supportive mentor or sponsor."[19]

Entrepreneurship and intrapreneurship are two additional concepts that many churches employ today, often without ever hearing of those terms. Entrepreneurship involves the establishment of a new business in society. Intrapreneurship involves the establishment of a new business or venture from within an existing company. Many of today's churches are beginning ministries that meet current needs within their own congregations while others are starting ministries to meet needs in their communities, often involving some personnel from outside of their own congregations. Entrepreneurships might include day-care centers, gang ministries, care-giver ministries, after-school tutoring programs, and parents' day out ministries. Intrapreneurships might include homebound ministries, spiritual development ministries, and educational ministries. As you can see, the lines between the two types of ministries may break down depending upon the target of the audience and the level of community interaction. Middle judicatories can assist local churches in starting both entrepreneurships and intrapreneurships for ministry.

Gifted leadership gives rise to self-starters and even self-managers. "Throughout corporate America, there is evidence that people are increasingly expected to manage themselves."[20] In the corporate world this is called self-management. In the church it is called the "priesthood of all believers" and involves the notion that each congregant is free to interpret matters of faith according to his or her own conscience, free to carry out his or her own ministries, and free to deepen a personal relationship with God. There appears to be new emphasis on the "priesthood of the believer" concept, a trend that supports the shift toward gifted leadership.

Anecdotal Support

An Example of Official Leadership

I recently visited one of our church members in an out-of-town hospital. This particular member seemed to know everyone in town and, as I soon discovered, out-of-town as well. She was awaiting surgery. As a pastor

I don't try to visit everyone just before they are taken into surgery. I have found that a home visit a day or two prior to surgery results in a better conversation. But this time, because the home visit revealed much anxiety, I decided to show up at the hospital, too.

While I was with her, she said "hi" to several people who passed by her room. The next group of people she greeted ambled into the room. They were from a very small community near where I live (in a very small town). After a few moments my parishioner introduced me as her pastor. The conversation immediately turned to church. This group of young men proceeded to tell me about the new pastor who had "strolled into town and tried to take over."

"He thought he owned the place," one of them began.

"Just because he had all of this education, he thought he could tell us what to do," another added.

"Every Sunday he preached about a different thing that he wanted changed. He really thought he was somebody."

"He tried to dictate to the schools, the neighborhood, the people in the park, everybody!"

"How are things now?" I inquired.

"Much better," came the reply. "He started working with the people rather than preaching at them."

"Are you attending that church?" I asked, expecting to receive an affirmative answer.

"No," they all responded in unison.

"But we might," one added. "He seems like he might just last a while now. And he's really not too bad, now that he's come off that tower."

Pastors and laity are beginning to forge a new partnership. Other styles of leadership, these days, seem to meet resistance rather than compliance.

An Example of Gifted Leadership

Reppa and Daniel Cottrell tell their story of modeling gifted leadership in a local church setting:

> We knew when we accepted the call . . . that this church was the #1

mission giving church in Rhode Island and that they desired leadership that would emphasize and generate the gifts of the laity. . . . It meant getting out of the spotlight ourselves and permitting Christ to renew the church. . . . Loving, listening, and learning have been the gifts moving us forward.[21]

Gifted leadership can also be modeled within a district, diocese, or synod:

In 1985, Rev. Neal Boese was asked to take charge of a program of evangelism and growth. He began his job not by sending out a mailing of all the great ideas and programs he had. . . . Instead, he spent his first months visiting every pastor in the synod, listening to their concerns and discerning what was needed in evangelism.[22]

The Pastoral Consultant Model

I believe that the future church will develop many new models for pastoral ministry. For quite some time I have been thinking about the model of the pastoral consultant.

When I was called as pastor to my current congregation, the church had a history of employing a part-time associate pastor to assist with Christian education programming. After the second such associate had graduated from seminary and moved on, we asked the question, "What is the best stewardship of these leadership funds in Christian education?" We decided to put the resources into laity training. Today more ministry in Christian education is getting done than previously. Not because the Christian education staff was incompetent. Just the opposite. They were too good! It was too easy to leave the work to the professional.

I am beginning to wonder if my presence in this church as pastor seriously inhibits ministry. Has the church come about as far as it can in the ministry of the laity with a full-time pastor at hand? One month a year we have laypeople preach, and the laity lead several other ministries in the church. Yet the members are unwilling to be trained in certain areas of ministry. Even though most people in the church can see how the Christian education ministries have improved by releasing one staff person, I'm not sure they are capable of seeing how the same result could occur by releasing both staff people! I am quite serious about the possibility of churches functioning without professional pastoral leadership. The setting I am in, however, may not be the place to start. I do think that this model could be implemented under a different set of circumstances.

Let me propose a job description for what I call a pastoral consultant for local church ministry. A pastoral consultant would work with the laity from two or three congregations, attempting to train laypeople to take over every ministry within their own congregations. This is much different from two or three congregations sharing a pastor, where that pastor still does all of the preaching, baptizing, distributing of the communion elements, and so forth. In this model the pastoral consultant would train lay teams to take over every aspect of ministry within their churches: preaching, teaching, visiting, crisis ministries, funerals. . . . The pastoral consultant would remain as a permanent resource person for the laity and continue to offer regular training and continuing education events for the laity. The congregations involved would pool together to fund the position.

What churches would attempt such a model? Probably only churches with their backs against the wall. The promotion of such a model would require a great deal of education and advertising detailing how this is an attempt at improving the ministries of the church, rather than going backwards just because there is no pastor. Still the only churches that would attempt such a radical model would be those convinced that they must either close their doors or try a new model of leadership.

But there are plenty of churches in that situation! Many churches have gone from a full-time pastor to a part-time pastor in recent years. Many part-time churches are wondering how long they will be able to keep their doors open. Many churches that have had a bivocational minister for years have been unable to find another. Many churches have tried being part of a two-point, three-point, or even six-point charge and would love to try something else.

Where would the pastoral consultant come from? I believe many pastors who have had rewarding pastorates for many years are looking for "one more challenging place to serve"—but find there is no place to go. The large downtown churches simply are not there anymore. These pastors could become pastoral consultants.

These are the parameters of the pastoral consultant model. If readers implement this model, I would love to hear about the results—or dialogue further about implementation. Please contact me through The Alban Institute.

Other innovative ministry models have been successfully implemented in other districts and dioceses. The Episcopal Diocese of Nevada has implemented a model termed "total ministry" that encourages the ordination of local priests and deacons through alternative ordination pathways.[23] The difference between total ministry and the pastoral consultant ministry model is that total ministry is still position driven while the pastoral consultant model is laity driven. I suspect that several other models of innovative ministry will arise in the future. We are truly entering some exciting days of ministry involvement.

Theological Support

We understand from Psalm 68:18 that when someone defeated an enemy in battle, the victor traditionally gave God gifts. In Ephesians 4:8 we see that God has reversed this trend for Christians and now chooses to give us gifts, even though it was Christ who made salvation possible for us by defeating Satan. In 1 Corinthians 12:7 and 1 Peter 4:11 we read that every Christian has received a spiritual gift. Paul viewed the people of Corinth and Thessalonica as his fellow workers and laborers (1 Cor. 16:16; 1 Thess. 5:12-13). Peter encouraged people to lead by good example and not be a tyrant to them (1 Peter 5:3). Laypeople are called to serve, intercede, exercise hospitality, lead, administer, give, discern, and exhort.

Surely there are limits to the ministries of the laity, right? Maybe not. Acts 8:1 says, "That day a severe persecution began against the church in Jerusalem, and all except the apostles were scattered throughout the countryside of Judea and Samaria." Due to the persecution, people scattered in all directions. All the people? No. Just the laity. The apostles remained in Jerusalem.

Later, we read in Acts 8:4, "Now those who were scattered went from place to place, proclaiming the word." The scattered laity went about preaching the word of God! Had they been ordained? Commissioned? Licensed? How could they do such a thing? Yes, there is biblical evidence that the laity has performed virtually every ministry of the church, even preaching.

It will require a new understanding of success for churches to construct this new partnership between clergy and laity, possibly the kind of understanding of success that Moses had. I was always bothered by the fact that Moses did not reach his ultimate dream of entering the Promised Land. Then, one day, I stumbled upon Deuteronomy 34 and realized that entering the Promised Land may not have been Moses' ultimate dream. "Never since has there arisen a prophet in Israel like Moses, whom the Lord knew face to face" (Deut. 34:10). Maybe the Promised Land came to Moses every time Moses conversed with God. The promised land for tomorrow's church may be more about relationships, faithfulness, and spiritual maturity, than about sanctuaries, buildings, houses of worship, and lands of milk and honey.

Moses may have possessed a different model for success than the one I had imposed upon him all these years. Clergy and laity being partners in ministry will require the formation of new criteria for success. Success not gauged by the number of people in church, the number of people on staff, or the number of dollars received. Success gauged by the faithfulness shown to God through this time of change in our congregations.

Where We Begin

Discussing the Trend

1. Are some people in your congregation "more equal" than others?
2. What ministries are currently performed by the pastoral staff of your congregation?
3. What ministries are currently performed by the laity of your congregation?
4. Have these lists changed any over the last ten years?
5. Are there any ministries in your church that are "off limits" to laity? Which ones?
6. How does your congregation view your pastoral staff? Are they up on a pedestal? Are they viewed as professionals? Are they servants? How else are they viewed?

7. How does your congregation relate to your denominational offices?
8. How does your church relate to other churches?
9. How many of your members can name one or more of their personal ministries?
10. What type of church leaders (both clergy and laity) do you need for the next ten years of ministry?

Applying the Trend

1. Make a spiritual gifts survey available to the members of your congregation. Introduce it through a sermon series, Sunday school program, or as a cell-groups emphasis.
2. Make a list of the ministries in which you would like to see the laity more involved. What would it take to reach that goal?
3. Is it possible that your church will be moving from full-time pastoral leadership to part-time pastoral leadership? Are you aware of a church that is? Assist another church in hiring a consultant to help it accent the positive side of laity involvement during this shift.
4. I would love to see a group of churches attempt the pastoral consultant model described in this chapter.

CHAPTER EIGHT

From Segmented Programming to Holographic Programming

One of my great memories is of a trip to the Holographic Museum of Art while on a sightseeing excursion in Washington, D.C. This was in 1989, when holograms were still relatively new to society. (A hologram is a photograph that reveals its subject in three dimensions.) We have since witnessed their effects and seen them show up in movies, wristwatches, bookmarks, and credit cards. The holographic copies that show up in such places pale in comparison to the art I beheld in this museum.

I recall a countryside church scene that took my breath away. The scene was not only magnificent; it was also mystifying because of its three-dimensional characteristic. In this scene this meant that if I physically moved my head an inch to the right to try to see around the church building, I could actually see around the church building, unlike a two-dimensional picture.

Next my eye was drawn to a hologram of a microscope with its base positioned against the wall. I naturally walked to the point of the lens, where I stood about eighteen inches away from the wall. At the moment I reached the lens, the image of the hologram shifted to the scene of an insect as if looking through the microscope.

The beauty of holograms is second only to their metaphoric quality for organizational life—organizational and ecclesiastical programming. Here's why. I had heard that if you took any piece of an original hologram, you could reconstruct the original picture from that one piece. I posed this rumor to the curator working the museum. She confirmed the notion. I was elated to see my rumor transformed into fact. So to me the structural properties of a hologram are as fascinating as its physical properties. Technically speaking, a hologram is a photograph, taken with a lensless camera, where the whole is represented in all the parts. If a hologram is broken, any piece of it can be used to reconstruct the entire image.

In a hologram, the whole is contained in each part. Ponder that image for the church. Isn't that the goal of church programs these days? To have each of our programs meet a different need for a segment of society, all the while presenting the full image of the church—the full image of the gospel—in that one specific program? The goal of holographic programming is for a sense of the whole congregation to be contained in each program, rather than expecting each program to carry out a narrowly defined and disconnected task.

Where We've Been

Segmented programming involves offering programs to the membership based solely upon need or interest. In segmented programming, each program is treated separately. Segmented programming does not take into account diversity of membership or the identity of the congregation offering the program. When the members of a congregation are quite homogeneous, there is no need to take into account the diversity of the membership. Likewise, with a homogeneous membership, there is little need to promote the identity of the church through its programs because there is seldom, if any, conflicting of identities among the membership.

Segmented programming views each program as a distinct and isolated segment. Very little thought is given to the overall picture of the programs. And very little thought is given toward promoting a program in order to appeal to a group unlike the current membership.

At one time the church offered a choir program for people interested in music, a softball team for people interested in sports, and a Bible study for people interested in discipleship. In those days the church never dreamed of offering different types of ongoing Bible studies for groups of people holding different ideas regarding what Bible study should be all about. Certainly the church never dreamed of offering different choirs for groups with different worship styles and needs, let alone a separate and distinct worship service.

Increased Diversity

Until recently most congregations did a very good job of meeting the needs of their members. Congregations were not concerned about a sense of cohesiveness across their programs—for a very good reason. No matter what type of programs churches offered to meet the specific needs of their members, all of the programs contained a similar quality, because each of the members within the church was quite similar to the others. No one the church tried to reach was very different from the existing members. The church reached out to people just like those already in the congregation.

Times have changed. For the first time in its history, a church may be faced with the challenge of meeting the needs of a community group that is so different from anyone else in the congregation that the mere thought of reaching this group calls into question the church's entire heritage and upbringing. "How can we appeal to them and still be who we are?" many churches are asking. Today people of differing theologies, incomes, orientations, ideas about God, and notions for the future of the church may all be found in one local church setting.

In the past there was much more diversity across churches than within churches. Resources abounded describing what type of programs to offer if a church was a particular size,[1] in a particular location (rural, urban, or suburban), or belonged to a particular denomination (every denomination seemed to have a uniform theme or emphasis). As the population within each church becomes more and more diverse, canned programs will work less and less well. The adaptation needed to make a generic program work in a unique local congregation will eventually become too much for some pastors and staff to accomplish.

Unity through Uniformity

Churches have always been concerned about maintaining their unity. Rightly so. "There is one body and one Spirit, . . . one Lord, one faith, one baptism" (Eph. 4:4-5). But many churches have previously, mistakenly thought that uniformity was the only path to unity. As DiGiacomo and Walsh explain, "Uniformity is only the means, union is the end. Unfortunately, many people feel that uniformity is the only means for attaining the purpose of the Church."[2]

In the past members wanted everyone to be like them in order to maintain unity. "Leaders must attend all weekly services of the church," some people still assert. In some churches today this condition for leadership would be emotionally, if not physically, impossible because of the wide range of programs offered by a single church.

Segmented programming appealed to various groups—maintaining similar content and process in each program. Holographic programming suggests that only the essentials of the faith must remain in the tone of each program and allows everything else to be changed.

Why Targeted Programming Fails

Many churches have made unsuccessful outreach attempts to appeal to a particular segment of their communities. A variety of reasons are often cited for their failure. Poor management. Poor delivery. Poor quality. I propose that there are two primary reasons for failure in such instances.

First, many programs fail to understand the needs of their intended audience. Presuming to know an audience is entirely different from actually knowing that audience.

The second reason is the opposite of the first. The failure of the program may have had nothing to do with the new program or its intended audience. Rather, the failure might have been based more upon the lack of connection between the new program and the essence of the church. Try to offer a new program with no concern for the consistency between the new program and the current church image, and you're disregarding the church's soul for the potential addition of one more body part. This new body part may make it impossible for the local church body to function.

I want to be very careful here to try to reduce the potential misinterpretation of this concept. I strongly believe that today's churches need to try to reach unchurched people, new segments of society, people who know nothing of God or the church. But these efforts should never be viewed as isolated efforts. Not one program of a church can be totally unlinked from all of the others. If a new program does not contain enough of the personality of the church, the current members will question the validity of the program, and the new members gained by the program will think they have been marketed a false bill of goods.

Today the two main problems associated with church programs are (1) achieving cohesiveness across programs and (2) meeting the diverse needs across diverse groups. Many churches may sense that the cultural and individual diversities within their congregations are too complex to attempt to meet peoples' needs while maintaining any kind of harmony through traditional programming strategies. Churches need a new model upon which to base their programs. I believe that the holographic principle presents a new and effective model.

Where We're Headed

Churches have begun to develop their own unique programs to meet the needs of people within their communities. And many of the more successful programs could be characterized as holographic programs that attempt to hold two disparate ideas together at once: unity of purpose and diversity of needs. Think in terms of offering a wide variety of programs to diverse subgroups and people—but each program containing the quintessential elements of the identity of the congregation.

Maintaining a Core Identity

What makes your church different from all other churches? If you do not know the answer to that question, you should. But unfortunately the tools needed to do so cannot be written within the scope of this book. Callahan suggests that there are four foundational searches that go on in churches: the search for individuality, community, meaning, and hope.[3] This may be a place to start thinking about your core identity. There are many tools and exercises that a church can use in discovering its core identity. For further help, refer to a previous work of mine.[4]

It is difficult to program without knowing the answer to the identity question. Various churches may hold radically different identities, so long as each one is clear about the identity and keeps it in mind whenever it commences any new program, especially one aimed at reaching a new segment of society.

Don't try to tell me that your church has no core identity! Just try to change certain parts of your worship service or organizational structure and you will quickly discover some of the things people in your church hold sacred. Every church has a personality, an identity, a raison d'etre. Every church has a core. Every church has organizing principles. Some churches never discover what their organizing principles are, or even that they exist, until they try to implement programs in a manner contrary to these principles.

As you have seen, I like to talk about holograms when describing church identity and programming. Margaret Wheatley likes to talk about fractals.

> Fractal organizations . . . have learned to trust in natural organizing phenomena. They trust in the power of guiding principles or values, knowing that they are strong enough influencers of behavior to shape every employee into a desired representative of the organiza-tion.[5]

To use holographic programming, one must understand that every-thing is connected. A church cannot expect to start a program and expect the new program, or targeted group that chooses to become a part of the church, to have no effect on the overall mood and identity of the congre-gation. Wheatley asserts, "In new science, the underlying currents are a movement toward holism, toward understanding the system as a system and giving primary value to the relationships that exist among seemingly discrete parts."[6] Every program affects every other program. So all the programs should have a core to them and the core should be consistent with the core values and essentials of the local congregation.

To say that everything is connected is not to suggest that the connec-tions are easy to understand. There is no way to predict what effect a new program will have upon the identity of the church. The only cer-tainty is that it will have some effect. I believe in systems thinking with one major qualification: Systems are not easy to understand.

> You think because you understand one you must understand two, because one and one makes two. But you must also understand and." When we view systems from this perspective, we enter an entirely new landscape of connections, of phenomena that cannot be reduced to simple cause and effect.[7]

I would never advocate predicting what effect a new program will have upon a congregation and then adding the program because you are anticipating that predicted addition to the overall mix of the congregational identity. Programs do not have that type of predictive quality. Rather, I suggest knowing what the core essentials are for your congregation and then agreeing never to add a new program that goes against those core essentials. Program in ways that are consistent with your church identity, but never try to construct an identity through the programs of your church.

Meeting a Diversity of Needs

Today church programming is much more difficult because diversity has come to the churches. Everywhere we look we see differences. Church is different from society. People within one congregation are different from each other. People the church is trying to reach are different from current church members.

Holographic programming involves trying to reach diverse people with a holistic gospel incorporating both evangelism and social action. A church may meet the needs of a brand new audience without compromising its views of the gospel message. The gospel must remain intact. Its package and delivery, however, must be constantly altered and analyzed to ensure that the gospel is not affixed to any barriers that will inhibit its arrival.

> Steak is steak. Bread is bread. Coffee is coffee. But, there is a big difference between the way these foods are served in a home and in a restaurant. There is also a huge difference in the way different homes and different restaurants serve each of these items.[8]

No doubt there are people in your own community waiting to hear the good news of Jesus Christ—because it has never been presented in a style or language familiar to them. Have you ever been to a conference or seminar and thought "I guess I agreed with their philosophy, but they just didn't speak my language." Even though you agreed with their message, did you apply it to your life? Probably not. For practical purposes, feeling uncomfortable about the delivery mechanism is as powerful as disagreeing with the content. The task for today's churches is to discover a way for new people to hear the gospel.

For the lyrics of the gospel to remain the same, they must be sung in new voices, languages, accents, and rhythms. Some people feel that changing the gospel's format or delivery is changing the gospel. Just the opposite. If we fail to take the gospel to new people, people who are different from us, people who have new needs from when the gospel was invoked, then we have actually failed the gospel itself. The only way to present the same gospel is to deliver it in a new way. The same old gospel is one that reaches out to all people. The only way the body of Christ can function is to recognize that each part must function differently.

Statistical Support

"A 1987 Gallup poll found 94 percent of Americans believe in God."[9] A more recent Gallup Poll revealed that 96 percent of Americans believe in God or a universal spirit and that 90 percent believe in heaven. Sixty-six percent would favor nondevotional instruction about various world religions in their public schools. Americans believe in God, but do they demonstrate their beliefs through church attendance? No. Only 28 perent of Americans belong to a Bible study group. Less than half of U.S. adults attend church on any given Sunday.[10] Statistics show that people are not disinterested in God, but that churches have failed to appeal to people.

Appealing to the unchurched people in society has become increasingly difficult for congregations. Religious expansion was at its peak between 1850 and 1930. Ethnic homogeneity was believed to be a major cause of the spread of religions during this period.[11] Diversity in America has increased, giving rise to diversity within local communities and within churches. Many churches have not taken a good look at their communities for a very long time. Programming that ignores this diversity will fail to meet the needs of some people.

Recently sociologist William Donahue commissioned an opinion poll conducted by the Religious and Civil Rights Commission.[12] The scientific poll asked what Catholics in the U.S. most like about their religion. The number one answer was "tradition." What do Catholics least like about their religion? "Inflexibility." Catholics want their church to be more flexible while maintaining tradition. To the casual reader, this sounds impossible. To me, it sounds like a cry for holographic programming: maintaining a core identity while appealing to more diverse groups. By the way, it is those in the twenty-six to fifty-five age bracket who want most to see the church change.

I must admit that the denomination in which I serve has heavily influenced my thinking regarding this trend of offering programs for an increasingly diverse population. I serve in the American Baptist Churches, USA, the most ethnically diverse and some claim theologically diverse denomination in America. Our denomination is moving toward a point at which no ethnic group will comprise more than 50 percent. But as I talk to pastors in other denominations, I get the sense that other denominations are becoming more like mine in terms of their internal diversity. I foresee this trend growing as we move into the next century.

Theoretical Support

Consumerism Theory

The strong propensity toward American consumerism is driving the need for churches to appeal to the needs of people in their communities. "Some have argued that the individualistic underpinning of the consumer orientation is a functional necessity in a modern society of diverse life-styles and segmented life-worlds."[13]

Many claim that the church should not be market driven. Such a concern does not apply to holographic programming. Holographic programming seeks to appeal to the diversities of people. But it also urges churches never to compromise either the gospel or their own core identities, which appear to be the major objections of those against church marketing. So holographic programming achieves the same goal as consumerism, meeting people's needs without compromising the essentials of the local congregation.

Holographic programming is heavy on meaning, mild on method; heavy on content, mild on tradition. Anderson says:

Ongoing efforts must be made to determine the meaning words and actions have. Traditions must be revitalized with new meaning in every new generation. The essential issue is not the tradition but the meaning.[14]

Marler and Roozen add,

The data indicate that denominational executives and local clergy can depend less on tradition and social convention to people the pews. Indeed, American church attendance is increasingly influenced by a concrete, local connection and consumer satisfaction.[15]

Holographic Organizations

On a different theoretical note, Morgan and Ramirez take the theory of holographic programming one step further by suggesting the need for holographic organizations, rather than organizations that program holographically.[16] What would such an organization look like? They first of all describe holographic organizations by contrasting them with more traditional mechanical organizations. They describe mechanical organizations as networks of jobs all precisely designed to fit together to form a coherent whole. In a mechanical organization managers ensure that each part functions through rules, controls, and supervision.

Conversely, the aim of a holographic organization is to create systems that are able to learn from their own experience and modify their structure by designing new groups that reflect such learnings. So the goal of holographic organizations is to create more autonomous units, teams, boards, or committees, each containing a sense of what the whole is all about.

Anecdotal Support

I present an example of holographic programming: A church offers an alternative worship service aimed at a diverse group of people within its community, often a group the church has formerly failed to reach. The goal for this new worship service is to package the gospel in a way that will appeal to this new group while still containing the most salient elements that make the congregation what it is. Is the church known for involving laity? Is the church known as an evangelistic congregation? A discipling congregation? A benevolent congregation? How can a church reach a new group of people while maintaining its traditional ideals?

Whether it involves adding a new service or restructuring an old one, removing the barriers to worship is an issue for many churches. Hugh Ross notes:

> Some congregations are beginning to see that what goes on in typical Sunday morning worship services actually widens the gap between themselves and the people they want to reach for Christ. Some obvious examples would be taking the offering, serving communion, lengthy hymn singing, unison prayer, and responsive readings.[17]

As holographic programming would suggest, removing the barriers is only half the work. "Just as significant as the elimination of barriers is the incorporation of new features that secularists would enjoy and that would help relieve them of misconceptions and fears about Christians."[18] Drama, readings, comedy sketches, and film clips are all examples of new genres that can still portray a very old message. A friend of mine who once attended the Willow Creek Community Church said that he witnessed a clip from the movie *Wayne's World* on huge screens that lowered from the ceiling during the worship service. Obviously this particular church is finding new means to reach a new segment of society.

All denominations will eventually struggle with ways to make the gospel relevant. The Catholic Church struggles with delivering the core essentials to a diverse people with its latest catechism book:

> From the outset, some critics expressed dismay at the very idea of producing a universal catechism, preferring the diversity and particularity of many different national or regional catechisms to a single Vatican-approved expression of the church's core teaching on faith and morals.[19]

Choosing curriculum is a great struggle for many churches, not just the Catholics. Why not approach this problem holographically? Take some time to list the three or four core essentials that you want out of a curriculum. Then analyze various curricula with these essentials in mind. Then offer a range of options to all of your classes or small groups, confident that each choice still contains the essential ingredients that your church values.

Theological Support

The church is still on the way (Acts 9:2; 11:26). Somewhere along the journey, however, many in the church forgot they were on a journey. Possibly because the terrain lulled them into a walk of myopia or they lost sight of their changing surroundings. Today's journey for the church must involve a redefinition of its core and the constant inclusion of new segments of society. Two tasks Jesus did quite well.

Jesus was able to ask point blank questions to people he met. Never compromising God's agenda, Jesus tore away everything that did not matter and forced people to focus on what mattered. To the rich young ruler he said, "There is still one thing lacking. Sell all that you own and distribute the money to the poor, and you will have treasure in heaven; then come, follow me" (Luke 18:22). To the woman at the well, he said, "God is spirit, and those who worship him must worship in spirit and truth" (John 4:24). He exhorted Nicodemus, "I tell you, no one can see the kingdom of God without being born from above" (John 3:3). Jesus told his disciples the parable of the two debtors then told the woman who had just dried the perfume from his feet, "Your sins are forgiven" (Luke 7:48). Jesus told the centurion, "In no one in Israel have I found such faith" (Matt. 8:10). The woman who touched Jesus after being unclean for twelve years was told, "Daughter, your faith has made you well; go in peace, and be healed of your disease" (Mark 5:34).

If you have noticed, these same scriptures also point to the fact that Jesus constantly tried to draw in new segments of society under the umbrella of his love and concern. Jesus ministered to Samaritans, centurions, relatives, Jews, Gentiles, old, young, elite, disenfranchised, blind, lame, arrogant, etc. Jesus witnessed and nurtured new groups of people unfailingly throughout his ministry. This is what more and more churches are attempting to do today: break down the barriers so that new people can hear the gospel and experience a sense of community with God's people.

Where We Begin

Discussing the Trend

Identifying Your Core:
1. If your church had a slogan, what would it be?
2. What makes your church different from every other church?
3. How does your church approach evangelism? Discipleship? Ministry?
4. Think about people your congregation esteems most highly. Then ask, "What do these people have in common?" "What do they admire?" "Why do we admire them?" Are these findings consistent with other discoveries about your core?
5. What spiritual characteristics would you like someone to espouse after being a part of your congregation for a number of years?

Identifying Needs:
6. What are the common needs of your membership?
7. What are the unique needs of your membership?
8. Are any of these needs not being met?

Applying the Trend

Articulating Your Core:
1. Take the Church Distinctiveness Survey in the appendix of the book *User Friendly Evaluation: Improving the Work of Pastors, Programs, and Laity.* It is available from The Alban Institute.
2. In a special service, celebrate what makes your church unique.
3. Communicate your core to various boards and committees.
4. Whenever a new program or ministry is started, ask, "Is this consistent with who we are as a congregation?"
5. Music is an excellent way of presenting your core ingredients to a diverse audience. A friend of mine recently relayed to me an experience she had as a member of All Tribes Church in Oklahoma; various Native American tribes celebrated their commonalities through the beating of their tribal drums at a single worship service. In what ways might your church find a common musical thread to celebrate commonalities among your diverse membership?

Identifying Broader Needs:

6. Where are the gaps in your church attendance in terms of age, eth-
    nicity, income, theology, and so forth?
7. List the needs of all the subgroups that you can think of in your
    community. Beside each subgroup, list a church or agency that is
    ministering to that subgroup. Where are the blanks? Where can you
    enhance ministry already being performed?

CHAPTER NINE

From Secondary Planning to Primary Planning

For an event to be successful, it must be planned by the people who care about the topic. Sound reasonable? Many people think so. It is quickly becoming a megatrend in our churches.

Churches are shifting from an institutional type of planning process to a more passionate planning process. Planning an event in the near future? Need help? Wonder who you might involve? Ask this simple question: Who feels most passionate about the issue for which you are planning?

Where We've Been

Events are no longer being planned by people who care little about the event. For good reason. It no longer works.

Most people would agree that the purpose of an evangelism committee is to plan ways for people to evangelize. Most people would also agree that evangelism committees have not been tremendously successful in recent years. One major reason is that evangelism committees are usually comprised of people who love to think about evangelism, not people who love to do evangelism. The difference is crucial. The difference delineates between people who hold only a secondary interest in evangelism and those who hold a primary interest in the action.

Secondary planning is defined as putting together a planning team that holds only a secondary interest in the topic. Primary planning involves putting together a team that has a vested or primal interest in the topic.

There was a time when certain church members could plan on behalf of other church members. There was a time when church members could plan an event for community members and expect them to come. That no longer works for several good reasons, the first of which should sound quite familiar by this time. We're back to that same reason underlying many of these trends: Church and society are no longer bosom buddies. So there is a skepticism rather than an affinity about any event advertised by the church.

Going to a church event may still be the right thing to do (just like eating oatmeal), but that reason is no longer enough of a motivator to get people into a church. After all, don't you agree that oatmeal is a good thing to eat for breakfast? When is the last time you had a bowl? Recognizing that something is good for you is no guarantee that a person will consume it. Many people today cry out, "Dad and Mom didn't go to church events or programs, so why should I?" That same person may even think that Mom and Dad should have gone to church and should be going today. I may believe that I should go to church. But I will no longer attend a church event just because I should, especially if none of my role models are going.

Successful church events are no longer planned by bringing together representatives of various congregational groups who have little or no interest in the topic on the table. Many church events such as mission circles, men's meetings, and annual fund-raising dinners have lacked appeal for quite some time, but out of a sense of obligation enough people attended them to keep them alive. The problem today is that the people who attend church events out of a sense of obligation are fading away. So secondary planning is fading away with them. It was easier to be obligated to the church when "church" was the only social option in town. Today a multitude of events vie for people's time every week. If mission circles and men's meetings are to be revived, those planning these events must involve nonattenders in their planning process in order to learn how to appeal to the people they are trying to reach.

Secondary planning no longer works for another reason that relates to diversity. With less diversity within the church, one group of church members could easily plan an event for another. As the people in the pews have become more diverse, in terms of theology, knowledge of the church, socio-economic status, and in some cases ethnicity, it has become increasingly difficult to plan an event for others. It is difficult to fill in the alluring details about an event when you know little about whom you are trying to allure.

Secondary planning is fading for a third reason that relates to age. Senior citizens simply cannot plan an event for baby boomers anymore than baby boomers can pick out a mobile home in Florida to suit a senior citizen. Generations today are more different from one another than generations in previous years. Society has even invented names for their different cohort groups: baby boomers, baby busters, generation X, and so forth.

People born in different time periods would prefer different elements in many church events, but worship is probably the single biggest church event that differentiates age groups. People born before 1946 have very different worship needs from those born after 1946. People born prior to 1946 tend to view worship as meditation. People born after 1946 generally view worship as celebration. There was great cause for celebration following World War II, so the children born after that war grew up with a different view of worship than their parents. This factor makes it very difficult for one of these age groups to plan a church event involving worship for the other group.

Secondary planning is much easier to administer. Easier, but no longer as effective. In previous years churches would often ask a church council, a board of elders, or a diaconate group to do most of the planning. With the planning completed, these boards often turned to others to implement the plans. In transferring the reins from the planners to the doers, a lot of the direction, velocity, and momentum was usually lost, causing the wagon train to arrive behind schedule and pooped out.

Where We're Headed

With so many opportunities to attend nonchurch events, people will now attend church events only if they perceive that the event will meet their immediate needs. The only way to ensure that an event will meet people's needs is to involve in the planning process the very people you hope to reach. If it's a youth program, then the congregation must involve youth in the planning. If it's a senior program, the congregation must involve seniors in the planning. If the purpose of an event is to attract a new segment of people, the people whom the congregation is trying to reach must be involved in the planning process. Even if none of them are currently in the congregation!

Tasks need to be performed by people who are gifted in those areas and planned for by people who are passionate about those areas. Too many times in the past, congregations did neither of these. In primary planning the planners become the doers—the ones carrying out the event.

Examples of primary planning may be found in teams that plan events for local churches, in congregational long-range planning committees, and in denominational committees.

Planning for Local Church Events

When planning a local church event, many churches are beginning to involve people with a primary interest in the subject. If it's a worship event, find people who are passionate about worship. If it's a concert, find people who enjoy a good concert, and they will be able to tell you what distinguishes a good one from a bad one. If it's a barbecue, find people who love to go to dinners sponsored by other organizations. If it's an international mission offering, find people who care deeply about overseas missions.

Have you ever been involved with a worship planning team? Did the people on the team love to worship? I would venture to say that this factor had a lot to do with the outcome of that planning team. When planning, churches are starting to involve those who have a primary interest in the issue at hand.

Think in terms of specific task forces or ad hoc groups strategically formed to produce a group with strong interest in the topic. Task forces and ad hoc groups are replacing committees. Our congregation has used task forces to plan community dinners, building projects, mission offerings, retreats, Passover meals, birthday celebrations, community ministries, and youth events. We have not always involved people who held a primary interest or felt passionately about the topic. I wish we had. Our results support this trend. The more successful events have been those planned by people passionate about the issue.

A word of warning may be in line here. Bringing passionate people together can also cause problems. Fireworks, fights, and frustration, to name a few. Schaller exhorts church leaders: "Do not ask an ad hoc committee of volunteers to accomplish in several months what took that experienced senior minister at First Presbyterian nine years to design and implement."[1] When you bring people with a primary interest together in a planning process, their self-imposed expectations may take the opposite turn. They may zealously think they can accomplish in a few months what took others several years. Keeping their expectations in this stratosphere will be the problem. But if organizational dynamics are allowed to run their course, the product will usually be worth the growing pains.

Primary planning produces hybrid events. A hybrid is something with more than one source. Passionate planning often brings both insiders, newcomers and latecomers, and people across generations into an eclectic planning process.

Planning for the Congregation

Long-term congregational planning is different from planning for a single event, but the same principles apply. It should be done by people who care passionately about the congregation. The language is very specific here: Involve people who care deeply about the future of your congregation—not about their own personal agenda.

Primary planning is quickly reducing the range of congregational long-term planning efforts. Two factors are shortening the timelines. The first is geometrically advanced by the second. First, the congregation changes its membership routinely. Second, as turnover continues, the changing congregation is becoming more and more diverse. Long-range planning no longer works well because the team ends up planning for a congregation that will no longer exist in ten years or even five years. Plans that extend too far into the future become secondary planning rather than primary planning by definition. There is no way for people not yet in your congregation to hold a primary interest in the plans you are making today for your future congregation. The only solution is not to plan too far ahead.

There is another problem associated with distant long-range planning. Long-range plans that extend too far into the future prevent the congregation from being responsive to other opportunities that arise along the way. The very best role your church can play in your community in the next five years may not be foreseeable today because the community need may not exist today. Keep in mind that one reason congregations are changing so rapidly is that society is changing rapidly. Once a church commits resources to one program, event, or process, those resources (including people—talent and time) will not be available for other ministries or projects until the current program is complete. Never use up all of your people in programs that extend well into the future. There will be no way to respond to other opportunities along the way.

To the extent that long-range plans emanate from a primary planning team, they have a strong chance of being implemented. To the extent that long-range plans come from a secondary planning process, they have much less chance of being implemented. Ownership has always been an extremely important issue in the implementation of congregational planning.

Planning for a Denomination

I have had the opportunity to serve on a variety of committees in my denomination. The principle of primary planning holds even in this arena. The best committees to serve on have been those comprised of people who cared passionately about the topic we were called together to discuss. One of the best was a commission designed to restructure our denomination's board of directors. Sound boring? I'm glad they didn't ask you to serve with me! The committee was comprised of people who enjoyed designing structures, and, more important, people who cared profoundly about the quality of work produced by our denomination's "general board."

Where do you find people who hold a primary interest in your topic when your base becomes as broad as an entire denomination? Through networks. In the future, networking people in denominations will become easier and easier:

At some point in the distant future, cultural anthropologists may conclude that the mid-1990's became the season America got wired. Today, an estimated six million individuals cruise the major commercial online services.[2]

The information highway is an excellent place to find people who feel passionately about a wide variety of topics.

When planning for a denominational meeting, sooner or later the subject of conducting business usually arises and is met with a collective groan. I am amazed at how many groups still plan business sessions for other people, hashing over topics they no longer find important and should not expect others to find important. A few groups are starting to change their business sessions as a result of reading evaluation forms and listening to responses from members. Leith Anderson writes:

> Increasingly, when I am invited to a gathering, there are advance promises that there will be no agenda, no minutes, and no formal organization. Such promises are made because the conveners know it is the only way the invitees will come.[3]

This past year was the first time that no business session was held at the state annual meeting for my denomination. The explanation: We are not pushing back the business, there is just no substantive issue to raise at this year's meeting! The planning committee must have been comprised of people who like to enjoy themselves at these meetings.

For several years my association (smaller unit than the annual meeting) has not held a business session at its annual meeting, which is now a "mission rally." Good things still happen, related to worship, inspiration, and encouragement. And if some substantive business issue arises, it does so out of the interaction of those present, not because of some a priori notion on the part of a few. In past meetings we have formed a mission trip planning team, donated funds to worthy causes, and planned to roof a building at a church camp, all spontaneously.

Statistical Support

Church membership turnover is very real. Depending on where your church is located, roughly half of your church members have been a member of your church for fewer than ten years.[4] The trend is toward shorter and shorter tenures. Church planning needs to keep this phenomenon in mind.

Businesses have discovered the same phenomenon of a rapidly

changing audience and adjusted their planning processes accordingly. A friend of mine teaches at the Harvard Business School, particularly in the area of not-for-profit corporations. He recently told me that of the eighty cases they use in their MBA case study program, only three companies have "long-range plans." The trend toward more responsive and emergent planning is present not only in churches, but also in successful businesses.

It takes people to plan something. What kind of people are most likely to volunteer at church? George Barna reports that people falling into the categories of fifty-five or older, African American, and married are more likely to volunteer in churches. People less likely to volunteer are baby busters, single adults, and non-Christians.[5] A church may have a difficult time gathering volunteer primary planners for a ministry geared to people who do not regularly volunteer in the church. But don't let this obstacle keep you from "going for" primary planning. The results will be worth the effort of seeking out people who have a primary interest in the particular project or program.

Support from Praxis

Praxis combines theory and practice, and for this chapter, I have combined the sections giving theoretical and anecdotal support. For two reasons. First, theoretical evidence to support this trend of primary planning is closely aligned to personal experiences of mine and others. Also, I see that the theory of morphogenic planning, which I present in this section, is better explained through immediate application than by dangling the reader too long on a theoretical tightrope.

If we carry primary planning to its extreme, we would actually invite the participants of an event to mold the event after they arrive. After all, who has more of an interest in an event than the people who have just shown up! Believe it or not some have carried primary planning to this degree. Some leaders have actually begun to allow the group attending an event to shape the event as it goes. This is difficult, but a good leader can pull it off.

This form of primary planning might be termed morphogenic planning. Bear with me for a moment. You've made it this far in the book, allow me one sixty-four-dollar word, unless my editor removes it, in which case you will not read any of this. *Morphogeny* is evolution applied to structural forms. Morphogenic planning involves identifying the major components of a certain event and then allowing the process to evolve once the event is underway. Its opposite might be termed *assembled planning*, which would involve putting each piece of an event together and attaching a desired outcome to each component.

Morphogenic planning starts with a set of hopes rather than a set of predictions. Planning with a set of hopes allows new ideas, side-effects, and directions to emerge along the way. Ideally this type of planning allows the best possible outcomes to emerge from the process. Morphogenic planning requires leaders who are divergent thinkers—people who can make new connections along the way rather than trying to fit every new idea or suggestion into a previously defined slot or category. It also compels a leader to be more of a generalist than a specialist. As people who attend seminars, worship experiences, and congregational events become more diverse, the need for morphogenic planning should continue to increase. Morphogenic planning can be used at retreats, worship services, in Sunday school classes, and seminars, to name a few settings.

Two years ago my wife attended a week-long Christian education seminar in which the evening sessions were allowed to emerge from the daily activities of the participants. Kevin Rose, the creative leader directing the evening sessions, had a rough outline for the flow of the evening sessions, but the details were allowed to emerge from the events of the day. Each evening contained creative worship and experiential activities based on the happenings of the day. Each session was allowed to emerge from the planning process rather than be defined by it. Each evening the interest for what was about to take place was very high, as the audience recognized that they had been a part of the planning team. They were ultimate primary planners.

I once attended an evangelism seminar containing this emergent kind of planning. Bill Cline took the time at the beginning of the three-day seminar to discover the various needs of the participants. The needs were quite diverse and many were articulated very specifically. I was amazed at the disparate expectations within this small group. The leader carefully adjusted the seminar to match as many of the expressed needs as possible. I am sure it took more effort, but I am also sure that the participants, including myself, were immensely more satisfied with the content of the workshop. Bill probably covered most of the components he had intended to cover. Yet the components of the workshop constrained rather than determined the outcomes of the seminar.

Another illustration of morphogenic planning is storyboarding. Leaders in several denominations have been trained in the process of storyboarding, which involves taking the participants' ideas and weaving them into a plan through the use of narratives, feedback, and group participation. Within certain limits, the people present at a storyboarding session, not the leader, truly have control over the outcome of the planning session. Every storyboarding meeting begins with brainstorming. The items listed in the first brainstorming session become jumping off points for the next brainstorming session during the same storyboarding meeting. Participants even get a chance to vote on what responses they believe to be most important before they leave the meeting.

Intrapreneurship is another morphogenic example, the paramount in primary planning.

> Intrapreneurs are people with entrepreneurial skills employed in corporations. But instead of leaving the company to undertake their ventures, they create these new businesses within the company. The company retains the employee . . . the employee gets the satisfaction of developing an idea without having to risk leaving the company.[6]

Stories of intrapreneurs abound at IBM, 3M, and various airlines. There is even a school for intrapreneurs![7] Every denomination should have a school for congregational intrapreneurs. In intrapreneuring, people who have a strong interest are allowed to pursue it. Congregational intrapreneurship is nothing more than primary planning done by an individual. Churches should encourage individual members to start up new ministries. This is primary planning at its best.

For too long, churches have felt tied to their structures and traditional ways of processing information. Back in 1962 Alfred Chandler suggested that structure should follow strategy and form follow function, rather than the other way around.[8] William McKinney says that denominations are not so much structures as cultures. If this is true for denominations, it is surely true for local churches. If the idea is good and a passionate person is behind it, churches will find that structures are not nearly so imposing as they think. Primary planning will involve new ways of thinking and doing, new ways of bringing together people who plan for the future.

Theological Support

Facing Goliath, David firmly placed himself among the historic host of
people who have felt passionately about a project. Goliath was nine-
foot-eight, wore a coat of armor that weighed 125 pounds, and carried a
spear weighing 40 pounds. David's own brother thought he had shown
up merely to watch the blood and gore, similar to people turning out for a
beheading or a hanging. For David, losing would mean death to him and
slavery for his family and his country. He defied every obstacle to complete his assignment. David's motivation for taking this risk grew out of
his single focus: "Who is this uncircumcised Philistine that he should
defy the armies of the living God?" (1 Sam. 17:26).

Rahab, living atop the Jericho wall, risked all by harboring spies for
Joshua (Josh. 2). Her life and the lives of her family were spared for this
act. Later she became the mother of Boaz, Jesse's grandfather, and is
commended for her faith in Hebrews 11:31 and James 2:25.

Jehoshaphat was told, "A great multitude is coming against you
from Edom, from beyond the sea" (2 Chron. 20:2). What did he do?
Confidently, he first sent out the choir singing, "Give thanks to the Lord,
for his steadfast love endures forever" (v. 21).

When Hagar obeyed the angel of God by returning to her mistress,
Sarah, who had despised and mistreated her, Hagar was rewarded with a
multitude of offspring (Gen. 16).

"The eyes of the Lord range throughout the entire earth, to strength-
en those whose heart is true to him" (2 Chron. 16:9). The church needs
people like these to serve on passionate planning teams.

An Ongoing Word

Now that you have read about some of the changes that are taking shape
in congregations, don't just sit there; do something! Discuss the book
with a friend. Talk about your reactions with others. Raise the subject of
congregational megatrends the next time a group gathers at your church.
Form a study group. Remember that the purpose of this book is to serve
as a catalyst for dialogue. Its aim is to give rise to new conversations,
not to give a final word.

The fact that congregations are changing elicits fear in some. Hope in others. I see an opportunity to envision. No matter what the response, we all must work together. Every congregational member is called to give his or her all for the cause of Christ. Anything less will not do.

Perhaps the only constant in the days ahead will be the certainty that God does care about the church. Knowing that God is present has always brought tremendous comfort to people experiencing change. Knowing that the same God who brought the church this far will guide it into all of the tommorows that come is both comforting and exciting. For anyone with the courage to pursue a dream, tomorrow is always more exciting than today.

Where We Begin

Discussing the Trend

1. Bring to mind the latest event planned in your church. Were primary or secondary planners involved in the process? How did it turn out?
2. If primary planners were involved in the event in question 1, try to think of an event planned by secondary planners. If secondary planpners were involved in the event in question 1, try to think of an event that involved primary planners. Compare your results.
3. If a major crisis or opportunity for ministry occurred within your community, how would you mobilize your church to respond?
4. What percentage of your congregation is committed to serving on committees for more than two years?

Applying the Trend

1. Consider the next major event to be planned by your church. Make a list of people who feel passionate about the project or ministry and recruit your planning team from that pool of people.
2. Make a list of all the new people in your congregation in the last five years. Count them and compare that number to your current active membership. Do the new people comprise a high percentage of your current active membership? What implications does this give to your long-range planning?

3. Pull together a group of people who care deeply about your congregation. Brainstorm possible activities that your church could do within the year.
4. Plan a one-day retreat in your church building on your primary day of worship. Begin with a worship service and close sometime during the evening. Bring together a group of people who love to go to retreats and watch them transform your church grounds into a retreat setting.

NOTES

Chapter 1

1. John Elfreth Watkins, "What May Happen in the Next Hundred Years," *Ladies Home Journal*, December 1900, 8.

2. Dmitri Merejkowski, *Jesus the Unknown*, trans. H. Chrouschoff Matheson (New York: Charles Scribner's Sons, 1934), 141.

3. Andrew Greeley, "A Religious Revival in Russia?" *Journal for the Scientific Study of Religion* 33, no. 3 (1994): 253.

4. Ibid., 254-55.

5. Ibid., 258.

6. John Huey, "Nothing Is Impossible," *Fortune*, September 23, 1991, 135.

7. Ibid., 140.

8. John Naisbitt, *Megatrends* (New York: Warner, 1982).

9. Alvin Toffler, *The Third Wave* (New York: Bantam, 1980), 9.

10. Huey, "Nothing Is Impossible," 135.

11. Stephen Covey, *Principle-Centered Leadership* (New York: Simon & Schuster, 1992), 30.

12. A. J. Van der Brent, "A Renewed Ecumenical Movement," *Ecumenical Review* 43, no. 2 (1991): 175.

13. Norman Shawchuck and Lloyd M. Perry, *Revitalizing the 20th Century Church* (Chicago: Moody Press, 1982), 18.

14. R. Stephen Warner, "Work in Progress toward a New Paradigm for the Sociological Study of Religion in the United States," *American Journal of Sociology* 98, no. 5 (March 1993): 1044.

Chapter 2

1. Loren Mead, *The Once and Future Church* (Bethesda, Md.: The Alban Institute, 1991), 8-18.

2. Paul M. Dietterich, "What Time Is It?" *Transformation* (A newsletter of the Center for Parish Development) 1, no. 3 (Fall 1994): 1-7.

3. Douglas John Hall, *Has the Church a Future?* (Philadelphia: Westminster Press, 1980).

4. R. Stephen Warner, "Work in Progress toward a New Paradigm for the Sociological Study of Religion in the United States," *American Journal of Sociology* 98, no. 5 (March 1993): 1047, 1051.

5. Dietterich, "What Time Is It?" 7.

6. George Orwell, *Animal Farm* (New York: Penguin, 1946), 36-37.

7. Gerald A. Arbuckle, *Refounding the Church: Dissent for Leadership* (Maryknoll, N.Y.: Orbis), 68.

8. Mead, *The Once and Future Church*, 5.

9. Keith A. Russell, *In Search of the Church* (Bethesda, Md.: The Alban Institute, 1994).

10. John Naisbitt, *Megatrends* (New York: Warner, 1982), xxxii.

11. Robert Cueni, *The Vital Church Leader* (Nashville: Abingdon Press, 1991), 103.

12. W. Lloyd Allen, *Crossroads in Christian Growth* (Nashville: Broadman Press, 1989), 34-35.

13. John Steinbeck, *Of Mice and Men* (New York: Bantam, 1937), 5-6.

14. Allen, *Crossroads*, 14.

15. Ibid., 15.

16. Kennon Callahan, *Effective Church Leadership* (San Francisco: Harper & Row, 1990), 16.

17. Avinash Dixit and Barry Nalebuff, *Thinking Strategically* (New York: Norton, 1991), 17.

18. David A. Roozen, "Denominations Grow as Individuals Join Congregations," in *Church and Denominational Growth*, ed. David A. Roozen and C. Kirk Hadaway (Nashville: Abingdon Press, 1993), 17.

19. Ibid., 17-18.

20. Ibid., 29.

21. Loren B. Mead, *Transforming Congregations for the Future* (Bethesda, Md.: The Alban Institute, 1994), 8-12.

22. Penny Long Marler and C. Kirk Hadaway, "New Church Development and Denominational Growth (1950-1988)," in *Church and*

Denominational Growth, ed. David A. Roozen and C. Kirk Hadaway (Nashville: Abingdon Press, 1993), 86.

23. Loren Mead, *More Than Numbers: The Ways Churches Grow* (Bethesda, Md.: The Alban Institute, 1993), 41.

24. Cueni, *The Vital Church Leader*, 11.

25. Allan Bloom, *The Closing of the American Mind* (New York: Simon & Schuster, 1987), 82.

26. Frederick Mark Gedicks and Roger Hendrix, *Choosing the Dream: The Future of American Religion in American Public Life* (New York: Greenwood Press, 1991).

27. Callahan, *Effective Church Leadership*, 13.

28. Margaret Wheatley, *Leadership and the New Science* (San Francisco: Berrett Koehler, 1992), 5.

29. Quoted in Dorothye Lutgring LaGrange, "Priest Depicts Church of the 21st Century," *Criterion*, May 14, 1993, 10.

30. Cueni, *The Vital Church Leader*, 73.

31. "Martyrium Polycarpi: A Letter from the Church of Smyrna. The First Martyrology, in *Documents of the Christian Church*, ed. Henry Bettenson (London: Oxford University Press, 1981), 9-12.

32. Hans Kung, *Theology for the Third Millennium: An Ecumenical Review*, trans. Peter Heinegg (Garden City, N.Y.: Doubleday, 1987), 144.

Chapter 3

1. C. Kirk Hadaway and David A. Roozen, "The Growth and Decline of Congregations," in *Church and Denominational Growth*, ed. David A. Roozen and C. Kirk Hadaway (Nashville: Abingdon Press, 1993), 127-34.

2. Quoted in Steve Sjogren, *Conspiracy of Kindness* (Ann Arbor, Mich.: Servant, Vine, 1993), 49.

3. Kennon Callahan, *Effective Church Leadership* (San Francisco: Harper & Row, 1990), 14.

4. Donald C. Posterski, *Reinventing Evangelism* (Downers Grove, Ill.: InterVarsity Press, 1989), 120.

5. Callahan, *Effective Church Leadership*, 86.

6. Leith Anderson, *A Church for the 21st Century* (Minneapolis: Bethany House, 1992), 63.

7. See Charles Bryant, *Rediscovering Our Spiritual Gifts: Building Up the Body of Christ through the Gifts of the Spirit* (Nashville: Upper

Room, 1991); Thomas Hawkins, *Claiming God's Promises: A Guide to Discovering Your Spiritual Gifts* (Nashville: Abingdon Press, 1992).

8. C. Peter Wagner, *Your Spiritual Gifts Can Help Your Church Grow*, (Ventura, Calif.: Regal, 1979), 177.

9. Roy Oswald, *Making Your Church More Inviting* (Bethesda, Md.: The Alban Institute, 1992), 57.

10. Sjogren, *Conspiracy of Kindness*, 30.

11. Ibid., 25.

12. Callahan, *Effective Church Leadership*, 20.

13. Lyle Schaller, *Create Your Own Future* (Nashville: Abingdon Press, 1991), 83.

14. Ibid., 84.

15. Howard Snyder, *The Problem of Wineskins* (Downers Grove, Ill.: InterVarsity Press, 1977), 23-24.

16. John Naisbitt, *Megatrends* (New York: Warner, 1982), 42.

17. Ibid.

18. Posterski, *Revinventing Evangelism*, 113.

19. Timothy Morgan, "Cyber Shock," *Christianity Today* 39, no. 4 (April 3, 1995): 78.

Chapter 4

1. Lewis H. Lapham, Michael Pollan, and Eric Etheridge, *The Harper's Index Book* (New York: Henry Holt, 1987), 52.

2. Warren Bennis, *On Becoming a Leader* (Reading, Mass.: Addison-Wesley, 1989), 91.

3. Roberta Hestenes, *Using the Bible in Groups* (Philadelphia: Westminster Press, 1983).

4. Kathy Lancaster, "Singing a New Song," *Church and Society* 84, no. 1 (September-October 1993): 73.

5. Lydia Saad, "One-Quarter of Americans Have Changed Religious Affiliation," *Gallup Poll Monthly* 4, no. 319 (April 1992), 39.

6. Leith Anderson, *A Church for the 21st Century* (Minneapolis: Bethany House, 1992), 42.

7. Bennis, *On Becoming a Leader*, 45-46.

8. Patricia M. King, "William Perry's Theory of Intellectual and Ethical Development," in *Applying New Developmental Findings*, ed. Ursala Delworth and Gary R. Hanson (San Francisco: Jossey-Bass, 1978), 35-36.

9. Ibid., 38-39.

10. Ibid., 35.

11. James J. DiGiacomo and John J. Walsh, *So You Want to Do Ministry?* (Maryknoll, N.Y.: Orbis, 1993), 31-36.

12. Morton Kelsey, *Can Christians Really Be Educated?* (Birmingham, Ala.: Religious Education Press, 1977), 7-21.

13. Ibid., 15.

14. Lapham, Pollan, and Etheridge, *The Harper's Index Book*, 68.

Chapter 5

1. The forty-third thesis posted on the door of the Castle Church in Wittenberg on October 31, 1517.

2. George Peck, "The Call to Ministry: Its Meaning and Scope," in *The Laity in Ministry: The Whole People of God for the Whole World*, ed. George Peck and John Hoffman (Valley Forge, Pa.: Judson Press, 1984), 86.

3. Kennon Callahan, *Effective Church Leadership* (San Francisco: Harper & Row, 1990), 13.

4. Tim Stafford, "Here Comes the World," *Christianity Today* 39, no. 6 (May 15, 1995): 22.

5. Howard Snyder, *The Problem of Wineskins* (Downers Grove, Ill.: InterVarsity Press, 1977), 23-24.

6. Dietrich Bonhoeffer, *Letters and Papers from Prison*, rev. trans. (New York: Macmillan, 1967), 211.

7. Kennon Callahan. (Speech delivered at Christian Theological Seminary, Indianapolis, November 8, 1994.)

8. Bill Hull, *The Disciple Making Pastor* (Grand Rapids: Fleming H. Revell, 1988), 147.

9. Ibid., 148.

10. Snyder, *The Problem of Wineskins*, 136.

11. Stafford, "Here Comes the World," 24.

12. Steve Daman, "Holy War," *Urban Family*, Winter 1995, 10.

13. Dr. Tony Evans, "Leprosy of the Soul," *Urban Family*, Winter 1995, 9.

14. V. Clay Noah, "Churches in Renewal," *Renew News*, Spring 1995, 4.

15. Norman Shawchuck and Lloyd M. Perry, *Revitalizing the 20th Century Church* (Chicago: Moody Press, 1982), 107.

Chapter 6

1. David O. Moberg, *The Church as a Social Institution* (Grand Rapids: Baker, 1984), 1.

2. Morton Kelsey, *Encounter with God* (Minneapolis: Bethany House, 1972), 44.

3. Morton Kelsey, *Can Christians Really Be Educated?* (Birmingham, Ala.: Religious Education Press, 1977), 26.

4. Robert Barclay, "Apology for the Quakers," in *Documents of the Christian Church*, ed. Henry Bettenson (London: Oxford University Press, 1981), 253.

5. Kelsey, *Can Christians Really Be Educated?* 26.

6. Daniel Leiderbach, *The Numinous Universe* (Mahwah, N.J.: Paulist Press, 1989), 9.

7. Robert J. Wicks, *Seeking Perspective* (Mahwah, N.J.: Paulist Press, 1991), 10.

8. Kelsey, *Encounter with God*, 40.

9. George Barna, *What Americans Believe* (Ventura, Calif.: Regal, 1991), 169.

10. Kelsey, *Encounter with God*, 151.

11. Don Cupitt, *Radicals and the Future of the Church* (London: SCM Press, 1989), 75.

12. Ibid., 141.

13. Robert Bly, *Iron John* (Reading, Mass.: Addison-Wesley, 1990).

14. Kelsey, *Encounter with God*, 58.

15. Fritz Kunkel, *Creation Continues* (Mahwah, N.J.: Paulist Press, 1987), 187.

16. W. Harold Grant, Magdala Thompson, and Thomas E. Clarke, *From Image to Likeness* (Mahwah, N.J.: Paulist Press, 1983), 15.

17. John A. Sanford, *The Kingdom Within* (San Francisco: Harper & Row, 1970), 27.

Chapter 7

1. Martin Luther, "Luther's Primary Works," in *Documents of the Christian Church*, ed. Henry Bettenson (London: Oxford University Press, 1981), 193.

2. Kennon Callahan, *Effective Church Leadership* (San Francisco: Harper & Row, 1990), 3.

3. Ibid., 7.

4. Ibid., 8.

5. George Orwell, *Animal Farm* (New York: Penguin, 1946), 123.

6. John Naisbitt, *Megatrends* (New York: Warner, 1982), 107.

7. Celia Hahn, *Lay Voices in an Open Church* (Bethesda, Md.: The Alban Institute, 1985), 52.

8. Leith Anderson, *A Church for the 21st Century* (Minneapolis: Bethany House, 1992), 46.

9. Timothy Morgan, "Cyber Shock," *Christianity Today* 39, no. 4 (April 3, 1995): 79.

10. John Naisbitt and Patricia Aburdene, *Megatrends* 2000 (New York: Avon, 1990), 234.

11. John Naisbitt, *Megatrends* (New York: Warner, 1982), 108.

12. Norman Shawchuck and Lloyd M. Perry, *Revitalizing the 20th Century Church* (Chicago: Moody Press, 1982), 61.

13. Warren Bennis, *On Becoming a Leader* (Reading, Mass.: Addison-Wesley, 1989), 197.

14. Stephen R. Covey, *Principle-Centered Leadership* (New York: Simon & Schuster, 1992), 37.

15. Dennis M. Campbell, *Who Will Go for Us?* (Nashville: Abingdon Press, 1994), 9.

16. Tony Campolo, *Can Mainline Denominations Make a Comeback?* (Valley Forge, Pa.: Judson Press, 1995), 119.

17. Naisbitt and Aburdene, *Megatrends* 2000, 238.

18. Ibid.

19. John Naisbitt and Patricia Aburdene, *Re-inventing the Corporation* (New York: Warner, 1985), 84.

20. Ibid., 83.

21. Clay V. Noah, "Churches in Renewal," *Renew News*, Spring 1995, 5.

22. Daniel Biles, *Pursuing Excellence in Ministry* (Bethesda, Md.: The Alban Institute, 1988), 69.

23. Stewart C. Zabriskie, *Total Ministry* (Bethesda, Md.: The Alban Institute, 1995).

Chapter 8

1. Arlin J. Rothauge, *Sizing Up a Congregation for New Member Ministry* (New York: The Episcopal Church Center, 1983).

2. James J. DiGiacomo and John J. Walsh, *So You Want to Do Ministry?* (Maryknoll, N.Y.: Orbis, 1993), 14.

3. Kennon Callahan, *Effective Church Leadership* (San Francisco: Harper & Row, 1990), 63.

4. See C. Jeff Woods, *User Friendly Evaluation* (Bethesda, Md.: The Alban Institute, 1995), ch. 2.

5. Margaret J. Wheatley, *Leadership and the New Science* (San Francisco: Berrett Koehler, 1992), 132.

6. Ibid., 9.

7. Ibid.

8. Leith Anderson, *A Church for the 21st Century* (Minneapolis: Bethany House, 1992), 116.

9. John Naisbitt and Patricia Aburdene, *Megatrends* 2000 (New York: Avon, 1990), 294.

10. George Barna, *What Americans Believe* (Ventura, Calif.: Regal, 1991), 234.

11. Judith Blau, Kenneth C. Land, and Kent Redding, "The Expansion of Religious Affiliation: An Explanation of the Growth of Church Participation in the United States, 1850-1930," *Social Science Research* 21, no. 4 (December 1992): 329.

12. John E. Fink, "The Catholic League's Poll of Catholic Beliefs," *Criterion* 24, no. 43 (August 11, 1995): 4.

13. Penny Long Marler and David A. Roozen, "From Church Tradition to Consumer Choice: The Gallup Surveys of the Unchurched American," in *Church and Denominational Growth*, ed. David A. Roozen and C. Kirk Hadaway (Nashville: Abingdon Press, 1993), 276.

14. Anderson, *A Church for the 21st Century*, 147.

15. Marler and Roozen, "From Church Tradition," 265.

16. Gareth Morgan and Rafael Ramirez, "The Holographic Model for Organizing," *Human Relations* 37, no. 1 (1983).

17. Hugh Ross, "Reasons to Believe," *Facts & Faith* 7, no. 2 (Summer 1993): 7.

18. Ibid.

19. Sue Smith, ed., "From the Center," *Church* 10, no. 3 (Fall 1994): 3.

Chapter 9

1. Lyle Schaller, *Create Your Own Future* (Nashville: Abingdon Press, 1991), 55.

2. Timothy Morgan, "Cyber Shock," *Christianity Today* 39, no. 4 (April 3, 1995): 78.

3. Leith Anderson, *A Church for the 21st Century* (Minneapolis: Bethany House, 1992), 48.

4. George Barna, *What Americans Believe* (Ventura, Calif.: Regal, 1991), 243.

5. Ibid., 254-56.

6. John Naisbitt and Patricia Aburdene, *Re-inventing the Corporation* (New York: Warner, 1985), 63.

7. Ibid., 64-66.

8. Alfred D. Chandler, Jr., *Strategy and Structure: Chapters in the History of the American Industrial Enterprise* (Cambridge, Mass.: MIT Press, 1962).

BIBLIOGRAPHY

Allen, W. Lloyd. *Crossroads in Christian Growth*. Nashville: Broadman Press, 1989.

Anderson, Leith. *A Church for the 21st Century*. Minneapolis: Bethany House, 1992.

Arbuckle, Gerald A. *Refounding the Church: Dissent for Leadership*. Maryknoll, N.Y.: Orbis.

Barna, George. *What Americans Believe*. Ventura, Calif.: Regal, 1991.

Bennis, Warren. *On Becoming a Leader*. Reading, Mass.: Addison-Wesley, 1989.

Biles, Daniel. *Pursuing Excellence in Ministry*. Bethesda, Md.: The Alban Institute, 1988.

Blau, Judith, Kenneth C. Land, and Kent Redding. "The Expansion of Religious Affiliation: An Explanation of the Growth of Church Participation in the United States, 1850-1930." *Social Science Research* 21, no. 4 (1992): 329-44.

Bloom, Allan. *The Closing of the American Mind*. New York: Simon & Schuster, 1987.

Bly, Robert. *Iron John*. Reading, Mass.: Addison-Wesley, 1990.

Bonhoeffer, Dietrich. *Letters and Papers from Prison*, rev. trans. New York: Macmillan, 1967.

Bridges, William. *The Character of Organizations*. Palo Alto, Calif.: Consulting Psychologists Press, 1992.

Bryant, Charles. *Rediscovering Our Spiritual Gifts: Building Up the Body of Christ through the Gifts of the Spirit*. Nashville: Upper Room, 1991.

Campbell, Dennis M. *Who Will Go for Us?* Nashville: Abingdon Press, 1994.

Campolo, Tony. *Can Mainline Denominations Make a Comeback?* Valley Forge, Pa.: Judson Press, 1995.

Chandler, Alfred D., Jr. *Strategy and Structure: Chapters in the History of the American Industrial Enterprise*. Cambridge, Mass.: MIT Press, 1962.

Covey, Stephen R. *Principle-Centered Leadership*. New York: Simon & Schuster, 1992.

Cupitt, Don. *Radicals and the Future of the Church*. London: SCM Press, 1989.

Daman, Steve. "Holy War," *Urban Family,* Winter 1995, 10-11.

Dietterich, Paul M. "What Time Is It?" *Transformation* (A newsletter of the Center for Parish Development) 1, no. 3 (1994): 1-7.

DiGiacomo, James J., and John J. Walsh. *So You Want to Do Ministry?* Maryknoll, N.Y.: Orbis, 1993.

Dixit, Avinash, and Barry Nalebuff. *Thinking Strategically*. New York: W. W. Norton, 1991.

Evans, Tony. "Leprosy of the Soul." *Urban Family,* Winter 1995, 9.

Fink, John E. "The Catholic League's Poll of Catholic Beliefs." *Criterion,* 11 August 1995, 4.

Gedicks, Frederick Mark, and Roger Hendrix . *Choosing the Dream: The Future of American Religion in American Public Life.* New York: Greenwood Press, 1991.

Glasse, James D. *Putting It Together in the Parish.* Nashville: Abingdon Press, 1972.

Grant, W. Harold, Magdala Thompson, and Thomas E. Clarke, *From Image to Likeness.* Ramsey, N.J.: Paulist Press, 1983.

Greeley, Andrew. "A Religious Revival in Russia?" *Journal for the Scientific Study of Religion* 33, no. 3 (1994): 253-72.

Hadaway, C. Kirk, and David A. Roozen. "The Growth and Decline of Congregations." In *Church and Denominational Growth*, edited by David A. Roozen and C. Kirk Hadaway, 127-34. Nashville: Abingdon Press, 1993.

Hahn, Celia. *Lay Voices in an Open Church.* Bethesda, Md.: The Alban Institute, 1985.

Hall, Douglas John. *Has the Church a Future?* Philadelphia: Westminster Press, 1980.

Hawkins, Thomas. *Claiming God's Promises: A Guide to Discovering Your Spiritual Gifts.* Nashville: Abingdon Press, 1992.

Hestenes, Roberta. *Using the Bible in Groups.* Philadelphia: Westminster Press, 1983.

Huey, John. "Nothing Is Impossible." *Fortune,* 23 September 1991, 135-40.

Hull, Bill. *The Disciple Making Pastor.* Grand Rapids: Fleming H. Revell, 1988.

Kelsey, Morton. *Can Christians Really Be Educated?* Birmingham, Ala.: Religious Education Press, 1977.

———*Encounter with God.* Minneapolis: Bethany House, 1972.

King, Patricia, M. "William Perry's Theory of Intellectual and Ethical Development." In *Applying New Developmental Findings*, edited by Ursala Delworth and Gary R. Hanson, 35-51. San Francisco: Jossey-Bass, 1978.

Kunkel, Fritz. *Creation Continues.* Mahwah, N.J.: Paulist Press, 1987.

LaGrange, Dorothye Lutgring. "Priest Depicts Church of the 21st Century." *Criterion*, 14 May 1993, 10.

Lancaster, Kathy. "Singing a New Song." *Church and Society* 84, no. 1 (1993): 73-75.

Lapham, Lewis H., Michael Pollan, and Eric Etheridge. *The Harper's Index Book.* New York: Henry Holt, 1987.

Leiderbach, Daniel. *The Numinous Universe.* Mahwah, N.J.: Paulist Press, 1989.

Luther, Martin. "Luther's Primary Works." In *Documents of the Christian Church,* edited by Henry Bettenson, 192-97. London: Oxford University Press, 1981.

Marler, Penny Long, and C. Kirk Hadaway. "New Church Development and Denominational Growth (1950-1988)." In *Church and Denominational Growth*, edited by David A. Roozen and C. Kirk Hadaway, 47-86. Nashville: Abingdon Press, 1993.

Marler, Penny Long, and David A. Roozen,. "From Church Tradition to Consumer Choice: The Gallup Surveys of the Unchurched American." In *Church and Denominational Growth*, edited by David A. Roozen and C. Kirk Hadaway. 253-77. Nashville: Abingdon Press, 1993.

Mead, Loren. *More Than Numbers: The Ways Churches Grow.* Bethesda, Md.: The Alban Institute, 1993.

————*The Once and Future Church.* Bethesda, Md.: The Alban Institute, 1991.

————*Transforming Congregations for the Future.* Bethesda, Md.: The Alban Institute, 1994.

Merejkowski, Dmitri. *Jesus the Unknown.* Translated by H. Chrouschoff Matheson. New York: Charles Scribner's Sons, 1934.

Moberg, David O. *The Church as a Social Institution.* Grand Rapids: Baker, 1984.

Morgan, Timothy. "Cyber Shock." *Christianity Today,* 3 April 1995, 78-86.

Naisbitt, John. *Megatrends.* New York: Warner, 1982.

Naisbitt, John, and Patricia Aburdene. *Megatrends 2000.* New York: Avon, 1990.

————*Re-inventing the Corporation.* New York: Warner, 1985.

Noah, V. Clay. "Churches in Renewal." *Renew News,* Spring 1995, 4-5.

Orwell, George. *Animal Farm.* New York: Penguin, 1946.

Peck, George. "The Call to Ministry: Its Meaning and Scope." In *The Laity in Ministry: The Whole People of God for the Whole World.* Edited by George Peck and John Hoffman, 83-93. Valley Forge, Pa.: Judson Press, 1984.

Peters, Thomas, and Robert Waterman. *In Search of Excellence: Lessons from America's Best Run Companies.* New York: Harper & Row, 1982.

Posterski, Donald. *Reinventing Evangelism.* Downers Grove, Ill.: Inter-Varsity Press, 1989.

Roozen, David A. "Denominations Grow as Individuals Join Congregations." In *Church and Denominational Growth.* Edited by David A. Roozen and C. Kirk Hadaway, 15-35. Nashville: Abingdon Press, 1993.

Ross, Hugh. "Reasons to Believe." *Facts & Faith* 7, no. 2 (1993): 7.

Rothauge, Arlin J. *Sizing Up a Congregation.* New York: Episcopal Church Center, 1983.

Russell, Keith A. *In Search of the Church.* Bethesda, Md.: The Alban Institute, 1994.

Saad, Lydia. "One-Quarter of Americans Have Changed Religious Affiliation." *The Gallup Poll Monthly* 4, no. 319 (1992): 39.

Sanford, John A. *The Kingdom Within.* San Francisco: Harper & Row, 1970.

Schaller, Lyle E. *Create Your Own Future.* Nashville: Abingdon Press, 1991.

Shawchuck, Norman, and Lloyd M. Perry. *Revitalizing the 20th Century Church.* Chicago: Moody Press, 1982.

Sjogren, Steve. *Conspiracy of Kindness.* Ann Arbor, Mich.: Servant, 1993.

Smith, Sue, ed. "From the Center." *Church* 10, no. 3 (1994): 3-4.

Snyder, Howard. *The Problem of Wineskins.* Downers Grove, Ill.: InterVarsity Press, 1977.

————*Signs of the Spirit.* Grand Rapids: Zondervan, Academie, 1989.

Stafford, Tim. "Here Comes the World." *Christianity Today,* 15 May 1995, 19-25.

Toffler, Alvin. *The Third Wave.* New York: Bantam, 1980.

Van der Brent, A. J. "A Renewed Ecumenical Movement." *Ecumenical Review* 43, no. 2 (1991): 172-77.

Vest, Norvene. *Bible Reading for Spiritual Growth.* San Francisco: Harper, 1993.

Warner, R. Stephen. "Starting Over: Reflections on American Religion." *Christian Century,* 4-11 September 1991, 811-13.

————"Work in Progress toward a New Paradigm for the Sociological Study of Religion in the United States." *American Journal of Sociology* 98, no. 5 (1993): 1044-93.

Watkins, John Elfreth. "What May Happen in the Next Hundred Years." *Ladies Home Journal,* December 1900, 8.

Weick, Karl. "Educational Organizations as Loosely Coupled Systems." *Administrative Science Quarterly* 21 (1976): 1-19.

Wheatley, Margaret J. *Leadership and the New Science.* San Francisco: Berrett Koehler, 1992.

Wicks, Robert J. *Seeking Perspective.* Mahwah, N.J.: Paulist Press, 1991.

Woods, C. Jeff. *User Friendly Evaluation: Improving the Work of Pastors, Programs, and Laity.* Bethesda, Md.: The Alban Institute, 1995.

Zabriskie, Stewart C. *Total Ministry.* Bethesda, Md.: The Alban Institute, 1995.